THE MILK OF INQUIRY

[POEMS]

THE MILK *of inquiry*

WAYNE
KOESTENBAUM

A Karen and Michael Braziller Book
PERSEA BOOKS / NEW YORK

for Steven Marchetti

ACKNOWLEDGMENTS

The author wishes to acknowledge the editors of the following publications, in which these poems, sometimes in other versions, first appeared: *Antioch Review* ("Into the Lobster Bisque of the Sky I Shall Sail," "Lament," "Poem for My Son" [I and II], "Gaudy Slave Trader"); *Boulevard* (excerpts from "Metamorphoses"); *Descant* ("The Complete History of My Crotch," "The Complete History of My Brain" [I and II], "Infection"); *Gargoyle* ("History of Boys"); *The Kenyon Review* (excerpts from "Metamorphoses"); *Michigan Quarterly Review* ("Poem for George Platt Lynes"); *Parnassus* ("Hygiene Kit," excerpts from "Metamorphoses"); *The New Republic* ("I Tried an Ox"); *Ontario Review* (excerpts from "Metamorphoses"); *The Paris Review* ("Splinters"); *Southwest Review* ("In Pursuit of Lost Rigor"); *Western Humanities Review* ("Who Polished the Wood?," "Poem"). The author also wishes to thank April Bernard, Karen Braziller, Michael Braziller, Lynn Enterline, Bruce Hainley, Faith Hamlin, and Jacqueline Osherow.

Persea Books, Inc.
171 Madison Avenue
New York, New York 10016

Library of Congress Cataloging-in-Publication Data

Koestenbaum, Wayne.
    The milk of inquiry : poems / Wayne Koestenbaum
        p.   cm.
    ISBN 0-89255-239-5
    1. Gay men—Poetry.   I. Title.
PS3561.0349M55   1999   98-50497
    811' . 54—dc21   CIP

Designed and typeset in Bembo by Rita Lascaro
Printed and bound by The Haddon Craftsmen, Scranton, Pennsylvania
Cover printed by Jaguar Advanced Graphics, Wyandanch, New York

FIRST EDITION

I do not know who put me into the world,
nor what the world is, nor what I am myself.
I am terribly ignorant about everything.

— PASCAL

CONTENTS

I

II

III

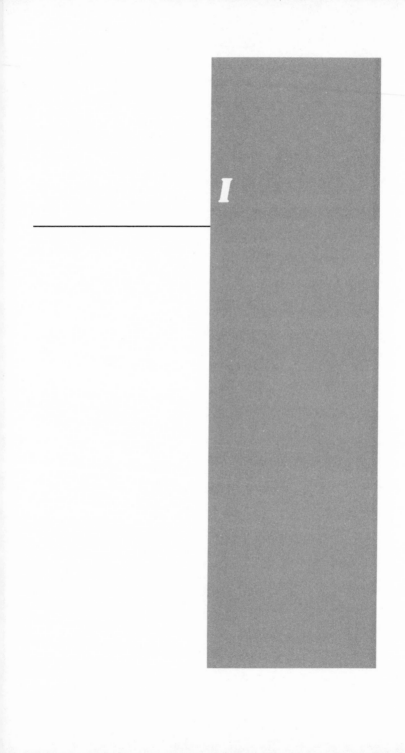

I

Forgotten Songs

1. Duplex

I left my mother's body
to enter a duplex.
Even she can't remember the street name—
a word in two parts.

I based my first poems,
ninth grade, on myths.
My parents bought me a mythological
dictionary, which I still use—

ninety-five-cent Bantam.
From nowhere a voice tells me,
"If you don't find happiness,
you won't be the first."

2. Broken Door

I broke, with my bike tire, a chip
off the blue
front door—just as, at birth,
I broke a piece

off my mother,
a piece off me.
Childbirth hurts
everyone concerned:

no one said
it was easy.
I must look at the broken door
forevermore

unless Steve paints it—
but he'll never find a blue
to match the original,
late in the evening,

all hardware stores closed—
so maybe he'll mix
a brighter blue
and repaint from scratch?

This is not serious—
just a tiny speck
missing. A wooden chip.
One door, marred.

3.   Soap

I slid like soap from my mother's body.
I stopped being soap in third grade.

Time is soap if you read about it, but not
if you experience it. Nothing you live

to narrate can be soap.
A castle is soap

while you cross the moat, but soap
no longer once you're in the dungeon.

I dreamt I was simplified,
folded, like a blouse—

I lay so still, so full,
I thought my season would never arrive.

4. Dalila

Dalila, with hard forearms,
was my neighbor.
I touched her muscles

and black skirt.
Dalila chatted with my mother
about troublesome kin.

I was almost in
time to be Samson, to tumble
down, a bowling pin!

5. Pragmatism

In a dream, I visited a quaint
Chicago apothecary and bought a teddy bear
whose genitals resembled licorice twists.

I prayed my recital would be cancelled.
Sure enough, it was. At eight,
exactly when the music started,

my mother stepped on stage
to call off the misbegotten night,
saving her son from humiliation.

6. Fifteen Peculiar Events

A small boy let gray turds drop
from his gray body at the fancy table.

Others attending
inwardly declared, "That's the 'gray' family."

Their underwear was gray.
Skin tone, gray. Turds, gray.

My level of organization
is superb today.

My double and I sat on a park bench.
When I called him "superb"

he seconded the compliment:
"I *am* superb."

My brother wanted to use the shower.
I said, "I'm showering now.

You may use the toilet if you wish,
but not the shower!" We're a firm family.

7.   The End of August

An extra in *Norma,* I tried to move
eloquently yet inconspicuously across the stage.

Accidentally I knocked over the set.
I remember the sound of the flats

falling. My father
had no part in *Norma.*

He starred in a legitimate play
about the history of the abacus.

A taxi dropped me off at its premiere,
though I'd given the driver no address,

no fare, just a miniature
rum cake. I pray this is a true story.

WHO POLISHED THE WOOD?

"Who polished the wood?" I asked Aunt Alice,
    though she was dead already.
Was I the boy she paid to help her clean
    rare cabinets of cherry?

Her furniture shone like shells,
    skulls, or stones turned to fossil glass.
I lifted a dust rag, squeezed polish from a tube,
    and set to work on the already finished task.

"Who polished the wood?" I asked,
    and rubbed the useless chamois back
and forth. But she was dead already, this suite
    of furniture a nightmare sent

by whom? No way to make the chairs and bureau
    shine like a legendary princess
mirror... I tried to insure
    the breakfront's discreet

demise by polishing it to death,
    but then my aunt decided it was time
to switch to lye, away from cream.
    "Who polished the wood?" I asked, but she

was deaf. I guess we were in hell. She lit
    a Marlboro. My mother said
"No smoking in front of the kids."
    Our lungs matured. A nipple kept on feeding me

the milk of inquiry:
    who polished the wood, and was it original,
or a restored, synthetic aureole,
    or just another Eastern European hole?

Alice's wig left patches of scalp
    to gleam, regardless of propriety.
At least she had the social polish
    to praise the cities that had kicked her out.

SPLINTERS

1. The Origin of Woe

This afternoon I met my woe,
    a formless sound.
I couldn't figure out her sex.
    Fearing my woe would run away

I shouted "Wait!" But my woe
    was out of earshot—
a malingering figure
    hunched on the horizon.

Undaunted by disease,
    I fell to my knees
and prayed. Bells clanged, and my woe
    returned, sweaty with fever.

I took a handkerchief and wiped the wetness.
    "Thank you," said my woe.
I swayed in the seastorm. Tied
    to the mast, I watched clouds scud

pitilessly across the blue.
    Salt air curled my hair.
The subway roared. I exercised
    a fantastic detachment and wore a reversible cape.

2. Telephone, My Mother's Ankle

I telephone my mother's left ankle
    this autumn morning
again. Everyone has a reflection:
    I find myself in conversation

with her left ankle, matching mine.
    You can't already know
the sound of a ringing telephone
    echoes my mother's left ankle.

I must have been an awful infant.
    In sunlight I see
the truth of my iniquity and telephone
    my mother's ankle.

3.   Roses Anciennes

The Jews lost faith in me.
    They never had much.
Ancient rose hauntings
    used to be stronger.

We who engage in documentary
    are often tired.
The man in the next world
    paints his walls

with a feather. The walls
    of his body on the fringe
of San Jose in 1970 near the underpass
    have gone away only momentarily.

4.   The Mother's Shard

No matter who you are, you open
    your heart to disappointment
when you touch a shard.
    Which? The mother's.

I have no shard at the moment.
      I want to wear
a V-neck sweater and never
      fondle shards.

5.   Neurasthenia

Normal, I live beside an ugly church
      and a vendor of fruit juice—
guava, mango. This is an ode
      to serenity. In the end

I doubt I'll call this anarchy
      my own. On the river,
reflected rooftops apologize,
      fearing persecution.

Are they palaces of sin? I thrive
      on denigrated
domino days, Monday knocking Sunday
      onto Saturday.

6.   Claustrophobia

I stand on the cusp
      of a giant undertaking.
Now I shall collapse on the floor.
      A twitching bird

dangles below my window.
      Of its import
I'm uncertain. I see
      a Deco stair?

I meant to go beyond the pale,
    and yet I'm still
well within its vast,
    staggered understatement.

7.   Transparent Flip-flops

I swam amid turtles in a pool.
    My arms brushed
kelp. On my feet, transparent flip-flops
    battled buoyancy.

My sister's absence and the clouds above
    the violins and court jesters
were forms of usury I could ignore
    until I left the wet

agora. I thank my lust
    for turning
away from cobalt immortelles,
    if they exist.

Aphrodite, lover of young boys
    and grapes, what
early hours I keep, though I was once
    your customer.

8.   Redwood Fence Splinter

Peony, aster, or withered carnation
    catapults me back to the redwood fence
splinter era: wandering down unsunny streets
    on Monday past the prime

I recognize Isaac in a natty gray pinstriped suit
        as my master. I have
no master now. No servants, either.
        I still burn myrrh

at shrines, out of habit, not necessity,
        not the root
drive I dramatized to the dense
        derelict nation.

POEM

Sometimes I think, to accommodate me,
the sky must become terribly naked.
And then I resent the sky. I wonder how it could do otherwise.
I pity the tugboat wandering in the west,
I pity the buildings afire with a commotion

that can't be merely individual,
that is fated to surpass the usual.
And then I begin to pity the airplane,
soaring toward Tokyo, and pity the clouds it cuts,
and I even pity the sunset, although the sunset is lucky,

luckier than I, for though I've mentioned sunsets once before,
then I meant a different sunset, less mature,
and now I mean the genuine sunset, the angry, petulant one,
which can't be tempered or resisted.
I pity the towers half lit and half left in darkness,

and I pity my listener, remembering her mother,
so difficult to grasp, and I'm not faking it.
I miss how slow the world used to be,
before I ruined it, this morning, with my crazy deliberations.
I miss the poisoned, old momentum of last night.

INTO THE LOBSTER BISQUE
OF THE SKY I SHALL SAIL

Into the lobster bisque of the sky I shall sail
with my mouth closed
so I don't say anything perverted about Apollo
whom I alienated during the last festivity.

Upon my honor
it was not my fault, and thus I transfer stock to Dionysus,
that randy fellow
widely known among the shades.

I envy the boy across the street
who plays airs slowly as if a tempo in his head
were also a tempo in the gutter
or the carnival, his mother's mind.

He knows his mind is not a carnival
and so he envies the hurdy-gurdy of his mother's.
I must escape all conversation with the boy
lest I corrupt him with my mutterings,

paternities, and sighs—
colors I spent my entire life trying to avoid,
as you must have guessed.
Listen to the importance

of having some thought
that makes the world less suffering,
even if the world in this case
is only your self, breasting the wind.

HOLES

My holes defy full knowledge—
I only rent my body,
and I don't feel at ease.

Wisdom, dim or clear,
leaks from the holes:
concentrated, florid hazards.

Holes are planes lined up
for takeoff on a military
airport runway. Is this accurate?

I like to return to places
I resemble. Rainclouds
condescend to me:

they have renounced
thunder, after three
ruminating claps.

THE COMPLETE HISTORY
OF MY CROTCH

1.

A few things
about simples.

I love the word "simple,"
meaning remedy.

I will open my heart
to you, fool reader,

if you are simple.
Simples sting.

May I offer you
a simple.

2.

A small favor I ask of thee.
I knew a thee,

her name was Mary Ann—
in a gold tent upon the river we exchanged

French postcards.
Elevated language is the mother of proof?

3.

I washed the new event,
a line. Shouldn't there be more
to it than a paper
cut, a solemn oath,
a very good
opportunity to eat
buttered crackers,
a fathomless
dinette counter
stool if you want
to be an actor
and twirl on it?
Soap, of its own
volition, barged
into my urethra.
I explained the song
to everyone, the screen
door to the side porch
slammed shut.

4.

My parents wanted to have children
and didn't want to have children—
both at the same time—
a thing so unremarkable

it hardly merits mentioning—
and yet I will mention it:
we fail each other
as worshippers.

THE COMPLETE HISTORY OF MY BRAIN

I love a pianist's nudity when I can imagine his mother
seeing it and thinking "My son has body hair now,
complex and beautiful, like his father, but more like other boys
I loved before I met his father,
or men I briefly glimpsed on Coney Island."

She observes the pianist's majesty,
the naked body of a nineteen-year-old Jewish artist
nervous about making mistakes.
At his navel, a few algae
curls bob, like pet fish seeking surface crumbs.

I have a crush on the entire family—
especially the mother's angle.
I have a crush on her leer.
But it is not a leer. It is a cold appraisal
of what she has created, of what she owns.

LAMENT

I want to stop being a person.
If only there were a choice—
a rat or signet ring
one could become—a waterfall

or the rocks the water lands upon, or an alien child
picking up a wet stone, drying it with a pocket rag,
taking it home, and placing it on his bureau top
so that other aliens can touch and admire it.

There is no choice, however.
I dare not answer
the knock on the door, the voice that says
Now you may become an alien,
the table is set.

Isn't it time to reconcile myself
to darkness in the kitchen, the confession "I have darkness,"
all whispered by one person, all forgotten?

THE BEAUTIFUL

The city stinks because of fungi
on the finest Pierian murals.

I must give up my addictions.
Marbled barbecue
beef in its foil bag. Lost
days, uninteresting and chalky.
The tropical optimism of the talk-show host.

The flapping, stupid birds
are not the Pollaiuolo brother clouds,
tumbling yet piled.

I don't blame them for their fakeness,
it's not their only claim
on being human!

O midges,
the city is sublime—
I will mime my admiration.

PILOT OF THE FALLING HELICOPTER

I've fallen in love with blankness, but the romance
has gone overboard,
even if blankness is a way of heading home—

down the drive, toward the indigo sea.
This sea, actually, resembles tar.
Someone must have set it on fire.

I rush to overtake the wind
on its way out the endless room—
if only I could find the chute!

I reproduce gloom
and then swim through it
in search of illusory islands, coconuts.

Before you ring the doorbell, make sure
your indifference has settled down,
a vagabond sleeping on the pebbled orient, after a day's
        winged lull.

Christopher Meets the Sublime

Christopher remembers meeting the sublime,
but now he is afraid of his future
and so the small raised letters on the sublime's forehead

fill him with premonitions of castles seen in picture books—
palaces along German rivers, a minor moat
crossed each morning by a genius princess.

I am interested in the princess
but must return to Christopher, who requires loyalty
without rewarding it. Staying in touch with Christopher
is like drinking a chocolate milkshake through a plugged straw

or like fading into horror—not facing it
but diminishing until my complexion
matches horror's, the two of us bathed in the same exploring
        glare.

Christopher is disgusted with the sublime
and has decided to quit his life of conquest.
Instead he will walk down lazar-house stairs
hand in hand with the genius princess,
who wears a magic cloak of immunity.

The leprous dukes stand below the landing
watching Christopher and the princess descend
in a virtueless light that threatens to slay its source.

My eye has pivoted in its socket.
The turgid river thrashes and foams.

Poem for My Son

The bird cried once in the brake.
I sang my throb note back to him.

He cawed: *None of it is about me.*
My song continued to erase him,

step by step: this wing, that orifice.
I longed to draw mermaids,

seahorses. I stoked his abnormality,
shifted his operating-room gurney.

All of him filtered out
through me: we

were fluid
on a rotten farmhouse floor.

OBLIGATION DAYS

Jesus preoccupied me in high school
but now I don't give him a second thought.

Sometimes my hand hurts, sometimes it
doesn't. I remember the gay student practicing

Chopin's third ballade; I waited, listening,
outside the studio. Again and again

he played one central, melancholy phrase
while I eavesdropped—an ambassador of deferral.

What obligations were deferred?
It's my duty to figure out

whether I'm among the damned:
i perduti. I remember how cold

the Polish church on the streetcorner
seemed; I walked past it on my way

to an empty apartment in winter.
I don't feel sufficiently nostalgic

about that dark month: I want to drive
a wedge between Thought A and Thought B—

in the winter of 1993
I was unclear. And therefore damned.

I never entered the church whose sign
advertised "Obligation Days." I never

met the student who played the third ballade.
I never drove that wedge between Thought A and Thought B.

I'm afraid of my own lack of intensity—
today unhappy I wrote on

January 13 and then *needs density*
but why is density valuable? What is density?

MEN I LED ASTRAY

The historian. The sociologist.
Now the wish to list the men fades,
the outmost clouds
wear ordinary rouge.

I wanted to rhyme "ill" and "will,"
but I conked out,
lost courage, fell asleep, and when I woke
I'd forgotten how to concentrate.

What happened to the autumn? I meant
to sleep away an entire season—
a speck of drama though I was
in an oceanic (Ossian-like?) sky.

I haven't said enough about the ragged sun,
its satisfaction in being the one to bind my life—
to bring the filthy pieces together,
on its way to more important tasks.

History of Boys

1.

Call him A
for angel butt, curved poplar—

the first butt I desired.
I thought, "This

is what sculptors feel"—
honest love of contour.

Butt wasn't separate
from boy, or from my consciousness.

Both—all three—walked past me.
"I could imagine touching it,"

I mused, but didn't push
the idea toward execution.

Religious, respectable, he recognized
my existence, somewhat.

Charity informed the butt,
made it a locus.

2.

M got a hard girl pregnant, sent her
to San Francisco for an abortion.

I imagined touching
his leg hair, bits at a time.

I didn't know how to go about it.
Without procedure

the action completed itself.
The leg felt hard, like a praline.

I had a praline disposition—
sweet, factioned.

Laid out on the floor
by my eye

he was no longer delinquent—
no longer the impregnator.

I decided, in fantasy,
to be kind to his legs.

The legs, then, might radiate
their own salt rigor.

3.

V's stomach crossed the hotel room.
He smelled of talcum

stick drawn across white bucks
to preserve their pristine suede.

The house he lived in
held V's stomach at night;

the house he lived in
faced a busier road than mine.

Lust played zither on my
belly's blank billboard, unlettered

marquee advertising no
good film, only some mystery about Malaga.

4.

Did F know his last name was a variety of bean?
His jock held nuts and other items, a safe

deposit box. He sat
on the gym bench; that angle

enlarged his bush. His grownup
name augured

grownup sorrow.
Looseness

suited the bush:
it had all day, all year.

No one—no girl—would ever discover
his pudge dusk stomach,

portions abstracted
from other contexts.

5.

The boxer flap opened, spoke
this humid moral.

GAUDY SLAVE TRADER

Everyone hates the gaudy slave trader, with good reason.
He represents the worst of humankind.

However, in certain moods I appreciate his gaudiness—
I'm prone to it myself.
Tonight I feel it return.
Can you advise? How might I purge myself
before it arrives? I remember a restaurant

with gaudy decor and exceptional seafood appetizers
in San Francisco. The restaurant will close,
or has already closed, but I stand here as witness
that it once existed.

I am not a slave trader but I am gaudy
is the only conclusion I can draw.
Even the act of drawing a conclusion
resembles weeping, the rheumy look my mother said she
        remembered,
and I didn't ask her when she first noticed it,

though she might have told me, had I persevered.
I never persevere. That is my first problem.

I should tabulate the problems,
but I resist tabulation.

One winter afternoon may be cold enough to change my mind,
but until then, resistance will be my only form of slumber.

IN PURSUIT OF LOST RIGOR

I'm no longer afraid of my unconquerable laziness, which kind
others have called "indolence," whether qualified
by the adjective "diligent" or "uxorious" is up to you to
        decide—
whoever you are, receiving plaudits from the circulating
        atmosphere.

So what if he called me "silly"—that man in the brown felt hat
with a paper napkin fastened like a tourniquet upon its top?
"Silenzio" cried the maestro, and I fell silent—but now you see
I've begun to speak again, my tongue an amalgam of flowers.

I'm not a clown, a tragic figure, an impressionist—
and any wish I harbor to correct misapprehensions of my
        motives
quickly succumbs to the undertow of a contrary wish
to continue ignorance's darkling reign.

I don't mind my resemblance to wine, and my longstanding fear
that all the tapestried minutiae I long to transcribe
are pebbles within the mouth of a superior Jonah's whale
abets my vulnerability to the "J'accuse" of a passing fly.

I Tried an Ox

Instead of a street, I asked if a lane would do,
or the soggy butt-end of a haystack-bordered highway.

I tried to ride
the dead man's ox but I feared the kickback
from the dead man, I was ruled by ornate phobias.

Hail to the rocks I didn't want,
and to the dead man's gift!
I shed all memory of the dead
and yet the river's boundary must be my own
as well, I can't surmount its flight to the far, almond shore—

the very shore I stand upon.
I meant not to hate the lifting fog but then it lifted
and I couldn't offer a sigh in response,
even if the waters, clearing so lightly,
imitated a woman who had given up.

POEM FOR MY SON (II)

"Sexually I'm zero,
but I've got a smart father," I smugly thought.
He told me about time's reiterability, about a girl
he knew in Berkeley, a girl he knew in Berlin,

a girl he knew in Cambridge (my mother),
a girl he knew in San Jose (my mother).
My father explained symbolism.
He siphoned smartness into me.

The man forced to be naked
dies a small death.
Already we were ruined, my father and I,
by the time he taught me relativity.

I knew exactly what shapes I wanted to see.
I wanted to be a prodigy.
There is no reason to go into this matter again
and again, except that it gives pain.

Dislodge my father
from my imagination and I
would have no imagination.
I would have a son.

My Child

My child has no
sex life, no sex organs.
Occasionally, an erection,
but these are accidental, and go nowhere.

"I'm sorry to plague
you," I said, and my child
replied, "Not at all."
Plague softened the air.

My child turns fourteen today.
I tell my child, "You look ten,
honestly," and we discuss
silver nailpolish.

I enjoy talking about makeup
with my child. I want to buy
my child a banana,
but it is too late,

the child's birthday is over.
I wrote a poem
for my child, what
happened to it?

The poem was in
quatrains. I haven't thrown
it out. Find the child
poem by midnight.

The Complete History
of My Brain (II)

Look down at my bare legs—their skin tone freakish
       yellow-gray.
Corpse light
reaches through the maple tree's leaf screen.

Object to the lack of hair on my legs but also protest
extant hair: curls degrade the skin, insult
the ideal of a smooth, neutral leg,

affront the intellect. Sparse hairs
frustrate the eye because they leave
visible so much unembroidered, unenhanced skin—

thigh without an imperial mission,
calf absurdly willing to sink
into subaltern status.

An observer might think my legs too masculine
but also not masculine enough: or else she'd be
indifferent to their hideous demonstration.

INFECTION

During my mother's infection,
my eyes brightened.
"Infection" held

just itself, the clamor
of denomination.
I admired the infection, and my mother

for containing,
housing, honing it,
preventing its spread

and discussing it.
Tasting its dignity,
I became more than a mere

album leaf; beholding
the room in which she dozed,
read, watched TV,

and gave directions
to the pimpled girl
who helped houseclean,

I stood in cordial, legitimate
cahoots with the grave.
My mother never specified

the infection's location,
cause, or symptom,
and yet it reigned,

sole object of regard,
and I paid fealty
to its custodian.

Son of the infection,
I formed some piece
of its magnificence.

I, though uninfected,
was the infection's
harbinger and scribe.

Hygiene Kit

Will love
tune the piano, swab
the cut evening?

#

Liz Taylor walked around an airport terminal
naked in a recent dream
her breasts didn't sink

#

nor were they beautiful
I followed her along a country road
she was hitchhiking

#

I gave her a lift
we had a duplicitous relationship
"we pretend to be mutually supportive

#

but secretly are adversaries" I confessed
on the phone to her and she said nothing
someone thrust at Liz a leaflet

#

of anti-me
propaganda clippings that proved
my badness

#

and caused Liz to turn away—
her laugh a crinkle
in cellophane

#

like my Mom's
mod face print dress
in its dry-cleaning sheath

#

"you're a hard nut
to crack" Liz said
and I, nut-like, sighed

Poem for George Platt Lynes

George Platt Lynes photographed a naked man, curled
          in a snailshell's infinite regress, and I want
to follow suit, my body a starfish seized
          by a Polaroid purchased on serious
whim: may I become the sailor
          picked up and froze in a print
hid at the Kinsey Institute until too recently!
          I see so many cuties on 23rd Street, they must be an
               industry—
members of an international underground elite
          gathered to plot the overthrow
of dogma—living replicas
          of Lynes's Orpheus, whose stubble
calls back from pandemonium the foreskins,
          pimples, and ingrown hairs, each paradoxical
nipple lit like Dietrich's angel—
          will I turn
pornographer? Before falling asleep I was terrified
          nuance would forever resist being enclosed
by a poem, however much it wandered from the point,
          so I thought, "Why not say this in prose?"
but then on waking reconsidered, and replayed dying
          Violetta singing farewell, asking Alfredo to give
her image—daguerreotype?—to his future
          virgin bride, whose arms, hypotheses, are pure—
take this picture and tell your girlfriend
          I'm now an angel watching you in heaven. . .
I fell asleep promising that when I rose
          I'd write a poem that did elaborate justice
to this world, but instead, in Rome,
          Sophia Loren, Marcello Mastroianni
and Fellini visited and refused
          to say what new film they were working on.

I begged, "Tell *me* before you spill it to the press."
      Sophia was singing Aida at the Met
and Colette hogged the parterre toilet—
      none of the nobility waiting in line had a chance
to urinate before the Surgeon General
      lowered the fire curtain on the Nile scene.
I am not a fake. I have two friends, three
      or four children, five fathers, and a host
of tropical fish. I never photographed Tommy,
      my first-grade friend who moved on Chanukah—
depressed pink light crimping the horizon's skirt,
      God mimicking Schiaparelli:
when I visited his new house, nothing was the same,
      the rooftop swept the sun
into green hatchets, and his bed abutted on a marsh
      I never had the good fortune to fall into,
else I'd now be giving you something keener than this sordid
      compromise between deceit and grief. At last
I have a playmate to rival that original, and plenty
      of cultural references thrown in, five-
spice powder, a predilection for the long walk, long
      haul, not much fuss, closure
kept to a minimum, and hyperbole reigning
      in her usual kimono, the color of merlot—
the silk one hanging in my closet smells cheap.
      Walking along the Hudson in 1977
beside an imaginary Balanchine troupe's prima
      ballerina, I saw, on a pier,
a man with top Levi's button opened
      showing groin hair, and I thought,
"Ditch the ballerina and follow this mariner."
      I didn't inspect his belly's superscript
or footnotes, nor the tattoo, serving notice
      like Madame Defarge, nor did I value,
at half her worth, the dancer, her navel bearing
      superior complexity, if I'd known how to see it.

A poet drove me to Philadelphia in a dream.
      Her mother disapproved of my defection
from orthodox practices, and I persuaded her that tapioca
      was a good idea for a dinner party; then my mother
walked onstage without warning during a poetry reading
      I was trying to give, and she said, "I'm sorry I'm late,
this is not normal behavior, but I have urgent errands."
      I long for a blue notebook
that admits every atmospheric tic, the despicable
      difference between *haute* and *bas,*
the small talk of my umpteen loves, my hand
      opening the window to invite
warm rain, and sunset tinting the street
      my father's uncle trudges up to bring a box of See's
chocolates on Christmas day—the uncle who married
      a Catholic, survived Germany,
then moved to San Jose to deliver mail:
      I disgrace the family by mentioning
graves and emptiness
      without also describing
ameliorative handkerchiefs
      and armchairs, philosophy lessons
and the Rubinstein concert in Caracas—"You have no irony,"
      my friend says, whose scarves are orchestral,
and I reply, "I have no sincerity." I used to weep
      after every haircut, smothered by uncertainty—
which look did I want, butch or meandering?
      "D'ja know?" is my new expression,
homage to Djuna Barnes—do you know
      what I mean, do you know what I seek, do you know
duration will not redistribute its fathoms,
      and do you greet the sky's openness
to opium as if its saturnalian curriculum
      made you and me
the sole descendants of the Ballets Russes?
      Before quitting

(accept this photograph, dear, and know
      that an angel gazes down on your happiness)
promise you will not destroy the magic net
      the marooned December moon
casts over casual thought; promise you will give moments
      on odd afternoons for the pleasure
a photograph allows—the Rudy Burckhardt shot
      of a solitary Brooklyn studio, its few faint
artifacts fastidiously arranged on a table—a room
      that might have been my mother's, had her childhood
looked out to the Bridge rather than to my own parched
            future birth,
      and had she worn clean oxfords in the old photo
I kept on my dormitory wall (her face pushing
      against her brother's chest)
beside an index card's typed Pound quote
      about the immorality of not staring the subject
straight in the eye, or else about Gaudier-Brzeska,
      dead in the Great War—
had she worn not unlaced boots but clean smackers,
      a kind of giggly shoe
that John Bunny, best fat comedian of the silent screen,
      might have longed for,
were he to lose the girth that made him famous;
      and promise I will not curtail
memory's melisma into the false carnival
      float shapes I have pursued for too many years—
Prendi, quest'è l'immagine de' miei passati giorni—
      squandered days in a whirling cyclone downstream,
who dares capture or call you home before the figure, nude
      on the silver plate that oversees these lines,
raises his hand to feel the fine light fail?

The Photographer

I took a photograph of my mother in 1965,
developed it, and now can see her face,
aloof or attentive or something in between,
as I am both. Incomprehensible.

This poem will tell you what I feel
about a simple photograph. Another poem
will listen, now, to the murmuring wind, which carries
the catastrophic quiet of a nearby highway—

sometimes the sound of automobiles but then suddenly
no sound at all, not even the simulation
of a cricket's chirp. Although it has already stopped,
I will not ask that murmuring to stop again.

THREE DISAPPEARANCES

1.

"I have been emptied already,"
I thought. "Why must
the emptying continue?"

2.

More deserves to be said on this front.
My knowledge of love
dissolves into a fine powder
the wind blows away.

3.

A balloon is rising toward the sky,
and floating above the river,
where balloons belong—and now it is dropping downward
again onto the despicable avenue.
Should we rush after the balloon?

Its episode of agony is over.
The air that once filled the balloon
with arrogant aspiration has vanished
down a cramped underground passageway.

LITHIUM

I have stopped thinking about lithium
and have returned to the Midwest, a cold state
north of a fragmented lake.

The pieces of ice are discordant. Each
may be a patch of music—a Spanish waltz, a French pause.

I have put down my camera for the moment.
I don't want to take
the picture—no matter how green the pine tree at the
    window's edge.

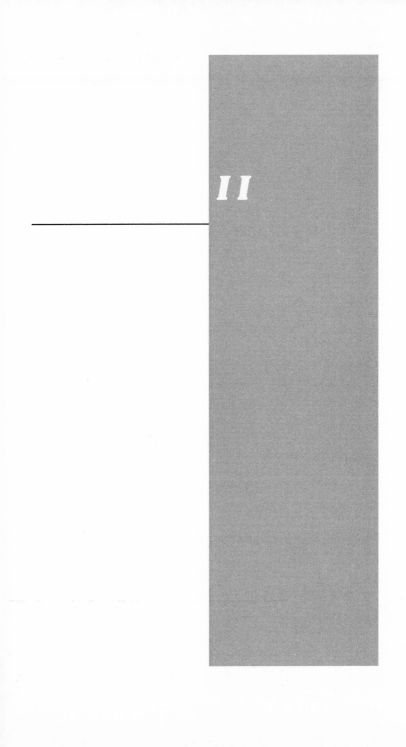

II

Four Lemon Drops

1. Lemon Drops

lemon drops in a letter by Dickinson
Hollywood single bed in a letter by O'Hara
decrescendo in a sonata by Beethoven
blankness in a life by me

Life with Bloke is what I'll call my novel
I'll be Bloke but you'll also be Bloke
we'll both be Bloke
two Blokes

Bloke took out the garbage
Bloke fed the cat
Bloke bought chèvre
Bloke missed my call

how many laps did I swim today?
how many boys did I desire tonight?
it's not easy to write a poem in English
no matter how huge your page

talked to Maureen, Frank's sister, for an hour
about his letter to Schuyler
maybe I'm becoming post facto New York School
although I live in New Haven

I don't care what people think of me
I'm not me
I'm Rita Hayworth or Linda Darnell
an Apache warrior

a cake of muguet soap
or rose or tilleul or carnation
I'm no known soap
no parfum

lady next door died a month before I knew it
think of the silent days she was dead, I not aware of her demise
passing her house I believed
she was still sewing or kvetching inside

phone conversation with my mother last night
we talked about her "botched eye operation"
and recipes and my brother's boyfriend and what life
was like for her at age three and my proficiency or lack thereof in
        French and whether gifts collide

Joe saw the fifteenth handsomest guy in the world at North
        Haven Furniture Works
but #15 is married or has girlfriend
"enumeration" said the poet "you like enumeration"
"yes" I said, her name was Tall

honestly an essay about Willa Cather would be entertaining
if I could discuss her valedictory speech about vivisection
"in defense of vivisection" by William Cather
an essay about Cather with asides about Stein would be
        entertaining but it won't be written, except here

heat wave dissipated to 60 degrees
no difference between two years old and thirty-five, woke up
        hating myself
went to sleep hating myself, pith of hatred faded at morn
when I said "I will have a milky breakfast"

truly I'm a weird guy, never nice enough to my father, never
      wrote a nice
letter to my mother describing her contributions to my weal
if I were to give up self-belittlement I'd have no other occupation
two years ago I wasn't looking out this window

need mystic language so I can deserve existence
language lightly
falls on New Haven backyard, dahlia, tar roof, failed plumbing
failed life dead lady next door

so what if I'm not tarmac drinking rain?
cute three-year-old Levine kid called my blue watchdial glow
      "minty"
I wish off the bat I could list three hundred people who
      know me
or just list three hundred people, period—David Cassidy
      Shirley Jones Billie

Jean King Billie Holiday Billy Ruane Billy Goat
Francis Ponge Arthur Rimbaud Artur
Rubinstein Glenn Gould Ljuba Welitsch Julie Christie
my household names Jean Genet Elizabeth

Taylor Faye Dunaway Edmund Spenser Frost
Hawthorne Dickinson Clementi Saint
Teresa Saint Sebastian William Cather M.D. Anouk Aimée
if I were to speak to you from my feminine floating island I'd say

I piddle away time
I play first Beethoven sonata
I run dishwasher
I train fan onto my ankles

I sign up for swimming
I lock locker
I undress
I greet roses

I eat niçoise olives
pickled anchovies
if I were with child I'd be witty about it
rainfall is silence between words

listen to rain
tamp tamp on oak leaves
telephone lines bearded sumac
I want to stop talking for a minute and hear the rain

is it a symptom of middle age to be beguiled
by silence, to find it
worth comment
or is silence disaffection?

a bit of both
bottommost thought is why am I divided
whom have I failed
whose failure have I forged

I don't want to know what I'm forging, I want to glide
past accommodations ampler than I've guessed
dumb bird amidst drizzle
says "grief," its sole vocabulary

in the few moments of silence you have left
name the bird the grief
the drizzle the avenue the reason
for continuing to speak

2.   L'Heure Bleue

rosé from Côtes de Provence and laundry
head uncluttered
I've foresworn envy
dreamt last night of Chopin Polonaise

envy's objective correlative
clematis fuller than I predicted or deserve
do I deserve to be alive?
do I deserve to escape skin cancer (knock on wood)?

I'm satisfied but do I deserve my lot and why do I wake in
        horror, sun in my eyes through opened blind
in *The Only Game in Town* starring Elizabeth Taylor and
        Warren Beatty why is she
both beautiful and ridiculous
does she have rheumatoid arthritis?

Aix
Arles
St-Rémy
Venasque

four Provençal towns visited
and now I'm home again without the proper joie de vivre
which means I should do charitable work
instead of grousing

sat beneath delphinium's "porches of the soul," delphinium eyes
        watching me, clematis eyes watching
sun on left thigh, hair golden-seeming in light
as if I were Apollo Ulysses or a character from Exodus
suddenly wearing greaves

sitting among thorned roses feeling no thorn
guilty of gluttony
I've decided to purge envy
from my life knowing it's half finished, maybe I've only ten
        more years

can't be greedy
Keats asked for ten, didn't get them
I call Steve "tilleul-head" cuz his head's full of tilleul thoughts
he calls me Charles cuz my head's full of Charles molecules

America's Two Queens
no more adoration of a solitary star
I must diversify my adoration portfolio
if I wish to blossom

L'Heure Bleue by Guerlain
Jicky by Guerlain
Jean Rhys mentions L'Heure Bleue
so do I

I tried to count to 100 in French, succeeded
I'm "into" poems also not "into" poems
if language is a record groove, I'm the needle
yclept Bloke

simple sentences aren't a crime?
gay guy nextdoor coughs
mailman has leprosy, missing fingers, stubs
intoxicating breeze makes me three years old

world hates me
I hate world
imagine year not organized into months
imagine year a fluid medium

no death no snow no sun no drought
imagine year a mother, imagine year porridge in the grown
        mouth
slowed down by what process of parturition or attrition
I almost said "amanuensis"

what is muguet
I asked the soap vendor in Aix
he answered in French
I understood none of it

is muguet honeysuckle or magnolia
Ronsard or A. de Musset
Nadar's photo of Divine Sarah?
we visited great Rachel's grave

in Israelite section of Père-Lachaise
I could write volumes
about shade across from Wilde's grave
girl sketching under tree asked "where is nearest Métro stop?"

we accidentally gave her wrong directions
we saw stones on Stein's grave
visited Bellini's grave *(Stranieri*
Sonnambula) Callas plaque in crematorium Chopin's grave

this morning heard Polonaise Artur Rubinstein careless
        immortal pianism
imagine world without valses
Père-Lachaise is the gayest part of Paris though saw no gay
        guys there
graves are gay

thinking nonstop about L'Heure Bleue, how to make more
        room for L'Heure Bleue in my life
tallegio for lunch
phone call from Maureen
discussed the words "honeysuckle"

"Buka" and "ALBERT"
is't possible to be somebody and nobody at the same instant
forget-me-nots rise thru bluestone cracks
careful don't step on forget-me-nots

I stepped on bee, reverie
Dickinson letters waiting to be read
don't like my hair, my glasses, my soul
I told the eye doctor "my hair hurts," he laughed

sunlight too intense outside
these words arranged on Firbankian orange postcards sent
        one by one
to Maman in Nice hideaway
whoever you are, you're a mistake

Willa Cather's interest in vivisection
a mistake
my interest in Willa a mistake
should I wear sunglasses while writing

alive at this moment and it (my aliveness) makes no difference
standing on sand in a timer turned upside down
foundation insecure
death's nearness means I'm nervous, weak

twittering bird
eyes smarting
I'm afraid of New York's monopoly on simultaneity
I want to be simultaneous, too

pulled shade brings
lupine Abbaye de Sénanque
sepulcher darkness
some honeys are milky orange

finger stinks of tallegio
tonight I'll wear Jicky, first time, Jicky's premiere
was Jane Austen ever antsy
did she ever say to herself "move on!"

move on to where
what zone name it I'll go there quick
sudden heat off tar roof plus elmleaf
dapplelight moves on

3. Negative Capability

head scooped out, no thoughts left
stillness in air proves I'm a baby
wish I had fan in this room, fan's in other room, that proves I
     lack immortal
Keatsian concentration

be not stingy to diorama's edge
parade on Sunday whom will I see?
what's a Neapolitan sixth?
I'm part of a fag generation

I respect fag poesy, once dismissed it
something faggy about poesy, period
lyrical voice recalling
itself at end of each line is faggy impetus

Carroll Baker suicide shoreside in *Harlow*
how did *Traviata Trovatore Rigoletto* emerge from Verdi mind in
     one spasm?
fold life in half, step into center's crease and make it a universe
met a guy yesterday who'd gained 30 lbs, didn't recognize him

"hi" I said to fat specter of old thin self
I like to bite the hand that feeds
sadist cicatrix
on middle digit

Cliff's mother's madeleines
can one call a cookie made in San Jose a madeleine?
can one be nostalgic for someone else's mother's madeleines?
and they aren't even madeleines

I bought a bag of madeleines in Paris, ate them in Père-Lachaise
on bench across from Wilde's desecrated grave
ate madeleine at graves of Chopin, Stein
wish I'd bought an extra bag so I could be eating a madeleine
        right now

sick of impediments in the path of happiness
I am not the only person on this planet
reading Dickinson's letters, reseeing *The Only Game in Town*
"I love you goddamn it!" Liz says

fine rain falling on tarmac
and if I became the women I adore?
befriend famous women famous men
when rain falls it drops, jumps up, first makes a career of falling
        then a career of jumping up

Dickinson saw particulars in brother Austin's arm
dreamt I ate goose paté with shrink
I balked at hardboiled duck eggs stuffed back into roast duck
        cavity
shrink's college friends eavesdropped on session

I wanted them out (get out!)
I was in P.E. class for short boys
it met an hour earlier than the regular class
after gym I cut math and ate goose paté with shrink

Ponge had good ideas
he wrote about soap and shellfish
why do I love to sightread rather than polish a single piece?
Beethoven is greater than I'd reckoned

sightread three sonatas
meet Kevin in front of the Pierre for gay parade
I am alone in the universe once again
just me and my voice and the air and the silence of late June

accustoms me to universal decay
torpor my favorite word, I used it in a letter to Rhode Island
stranger with huge hard-on that stuck straight out like flag or
      proclamation
short bald guy where are you this summer?

writing gives me a hard-on
that's what they say of Milton, "earned dignity"
what about earned hard-on
hardwon

I guess I want to shock the ladies
I'm a lady, too
in white gloves holding *Paris-Match* at Aux Deux Magots
      feeding water to my pekinese
I can only do so much to help the English language

in deployment of fag idiom I am not alone
in seeking continuity between mystical expansion and fag idiom
even Dickinson in her own way used fag idiom
old doldrums (sophistries?) of June

I write about longing
it's difficult not to depend on names of authors
I like dropping their names
it's as if I'm dropping their whole oeuvres

if you get rid of the period
then you destroy
expectations of the falling rose
I meant the voice falling

Fontainebleau rose garden two
black or white swans moving
toward castle and breakfast room alight damasked waitress
asking if I want "oeuf à la coq"

if I were a book, not a person, dear brother then I'd be you
everything addressed to Brother
middle-aged I for first time
sympathized with white emeritus flab ass

white lustreless pubic hair, pointless cock
no value in aged penis, penis isn't confit
in pictures my shoulders don't seem broad
ass too big

I'd love to befriend New Yorkers
artists with smudged eyes
like Janice, child I once knew
red stain (bruise?) near her eye signified individuality

I wanted bruised eye
the English language a rich possession
"may I send addleberry jelly" Emily might have asked Austin
        in a letter
it's too late in my life to make addleberry jelly

is my heart a locked ten-year diary?
movie stars should write poems
"saw Tom Hanks today for brunch, bumped into Sue Mengers"
it would be interesting to read Liz's poem about the perfume
        industry

she might never write that poem so I must do it for her
is it possible to befriend stars
I am more interested in proper nouns than verbs
dreamt Liz and I climbed over rough landscape toward subway
        stop

I have an unusual, well-nigh hysterical susceptibility to other
        people's forcefields
so though alone I'm surrounded by human entities
starlets David Cassidy, always David, Sean too
the Bonaduce redhead

I'm paranoid, it's names I love, ghosts, Mae
here in the room: Mae Questel Mae West Aunt Mae
weird having three Maes
at once in my flesh

like Cather I want size
no writer feels otherwise
I write because I'm afraid of space
and want to colonize

a friend saw Patty Hearst on Metro North
"her relationships so one-sided as to be almost hallucinatory"
that quotation, concerning Dickinson, interested Joseph Cornell
I hallucinate thee

no "vous" in this language to accommodate immanence
through gloryhole the cock's appearance is lilliputian or _____
a word of which I never tire
cute pornstar I met on the train telephoned

truly the cutest but no longer a pornstar
I was cold on the phone
not an easy guy to befriend
I must have a reputation for chill

I'd never known an ex-pornstar
his mother saw his hard-on
in a spread someone mailed to her
my spread's not Oedipal, it's literary

he swam in gay games
"no one from the team is talking to me any longer"
in the 20th century we have our own sultry desultory gods,
        among them Genet
who may not believe me

dreamt Ashbery gave me a book with obscure surreal inscription
was it an invitation, a seduction
or just his ordinary m.o.?
in any case I liked being close to J.A.

maybe because it's raining outside it's also raining inside
fuck quatrains
here in exclamation's midst
I don't care about autobiography, I only care about aggression

dreams and storms
drenched on way to buy nectarines, beans, eggs
Finnish spuds, curly onion bread
I noted shopkeeper's daughter's cleavage

becoming restless because of rain I don't want
my life to be a waste
Dickinson's wasn't
she spent herself

is the performance of my own personality a sufficiently
        abstract enterprise?
I said I'd retire, now I've retired
time isn't simple even after you've retired
reading Dickinson's letters on the cabbage rose couch I
        wouldn't mind a few lone moments to rethink time

4. Parade

topless ladies, men with thatch exposed, lowhanging sarongs
what did I make of bearded lady?
saw 4,000 men, did nothing
that's desire, you can do nothing with it

played late Beethoven sonatas
another day of waiting by the phone
for transformation
slept like the undead

"why am I always so unhappy I have no reason," quoth me
on phone
"mossy," past girlfriend
said, "you have a mossy voice"

does mossy voice mean
moonlight sonata
obsessive enumeration?
too many books

my mother used to read in bed
I remember the pillow she leaned into
and how her reclining posture symbolized intellection and
        repose
qualities I yearned for

intellection and Helen Keller and Radcliffe
the life of the mind and the life of the subway ride going
        nowhere
the life of no life
and my father eating herring straight out of the jar in the dark
        kitchen

Radcliffe, meaning lesbian (Radclyffe Hall)
where my mother's meanings went awry
where she met my father at hamburger shoppe
my mother beside me at *GWTW* at *Love Story*

at vanilla milkshake hour
my mother ordering steak at Big Boy while my father orders
        sole
because it's cheaper
I want my father not to go into debt so I order sole too

I wish my mother weren't extravagant
and yet I eagerly inherit her extravagance
obscene to talk about mothers in public
this isn't public so I can write in peace

at L's house watching her pubescent son
who probably masturbates two hours a day
I eat chicken on the love seat while she talks to me
how difficult it must be to masturbate in a house occupied by
      smart mother and father

father has big tanned tennisplaying nose
I'd like him to be my shrink
maybe strip him
can't strip one's shrink, however

must be difficult to find a place to masturbate in peace in that
      huge shrink house
smart father aware where boy's libido is going
smart mother also aware as she studies Steinbeck and Kate
      Chopin
serving tabbouleh to the masturbating son

most sons masturbate, no big deal
a general woe
I *do* have friends
must not scatter thought like seed on the recumbent sheet

I knew a lit teacher who walked into her son's bedroom while
      he was masturbating
she told me "he has a big penis just like his father"
this revelation titillated
and horrified me

imagine the mother opening
the door and seeing the son's mirror penis
the teacher who admires Welty
and Katherine Anne Porter thinking

66

"he has a big penis just like his father" then shutting
the door on the son's antic
what is the son doing masturbating at home at nineteen?
probably he is between girlfriends

does the mother feel proud or queasy as she gazes
quickly at the dittomaster penis
and then goes back
to her xerox of a Welty story about a worn path

dreamt I traveled with family to Genoa, Provençal hill towns
bought fresh donuts from a carnival foodstand
like Chez Panisse
lady toppled downstairs backward

was lady my grandmother
I wailed
I am relentlessly referential
just talked to Adam who has a sweet preppy voice in the
        Midwest

once he tied a necktie around his penis at a party and I was
        jealous
of his penile confidence
I wouldn't have the nerve
what if I got an erection?

I have no control
over erections
hence I don't skinnydip
I feel abandoned by my ladies

the ladies protected me
they no longer do
the ladies aren't strong enough
to shield me from time and flood

when I wake in the morning I wonder if I'm in France
I'm afraid I won't have a future
moment of silence for gone men and women
at 3 p.m. yesterday, gay pride parade

I thought of John
often I think of John
in Central Park in Paris (Marais) at women's boutique
in Avignon on rue des Teinturiers at the Chapelle des
      Pénitents-Gris I think of John

Avignon was his city
no longer will I see him sudden on streetcorner (Chapel, High)
pixie who understood danger and nature
not once has appeared in my dreams

I have few short friends
John, dead now, was my short friend
why should the future be a state of extremity from which I
      must be rescued?
the future isn't an obscene planet

or a virus
why do I want to be a poet? because I want to live inside my
      body while I have the liberty
while not in a state of siege
I want the pleasure of inhabiting my lovely body

before it decays I want
to tell you what it's like occupying a decent male body during
      this decade, now
wherefore am I so sad
lycanthropic Antonio said

melancholy's the Petrarchan sickness said my friend
a scholar of renaissance dolor
if I understood the history
of melancholy I might begin this poem properly for once!

in the meantime not knowing melancholy's genesis
I will tell you I am sad for no good reason
sick for a week in Venasque I counted syllables, they kept me
      reined in
time to take a drug

does my mother take drugs
I should ask my mother about pills
that would be a good conversation
Mom do you use dolls

Mom do you mind if I include you in poems
she wouldn't mind, secretly she might
it would be Mom-like to mind
and not tell me

lucky Mom alive to mind
clematis O you diplomat of kindness
and added to your bounty the muguet tilleul and rose sauvage
      soaps in the bedroom's wicker basket
and the Waldstein Sonata badly played, octave rush blurred

and fig bread, platonic
when these are joined I reconsider death
and change, deities I could visit include Dickinson's letters
letters I could write include this one, to the clematis

atwirl up fence we shared with now dead lady we nicknamed
      "Cha"
because of cha-cha heels? no, because of her last name, which
      I won't write down
won't tread on Cha's real name
Sasha invites me to swim past island rocks in Branford Sound

snob, I won't accept
I am a cold gilled fish
Lord I've asked for a few simple things and I've gotten most
    of them and still
some sorrow gnaws

reading Dickinson letters
in bedroom with rose soap
worrying about failure and illness
Dickinson didn't worry, she just existed in her fine time

her time finer than mine
currant wine
was one of her preoccupations
here is my time and I should be experiencing joy

instead all I feel is stale humidity
and torment and yet now in my eyes comes the soleil
blinding and adequate
O silence

I used to fear your steadfastness
Dickinson lost the use of her eyes
did she use eye drops
I know nothing of nineteenth-century medicine

fortunately no one is listening
so I can tell what passes
for truth in New England
if someone listens

I'll call it quits
in midst of transfiguration
watch my limbs turn gold
Lemon Pledge or lava

coating my arms and legs
as they attempt to move
quickly into the hereafter
the ordinary daylight of a work week

looks marvelous if you take it apart
it loses the speciousness
of romance
and takes on the solemnity

of a sacrifice I've long awaited
two bodies curled into each other
one retreating
the other advancing

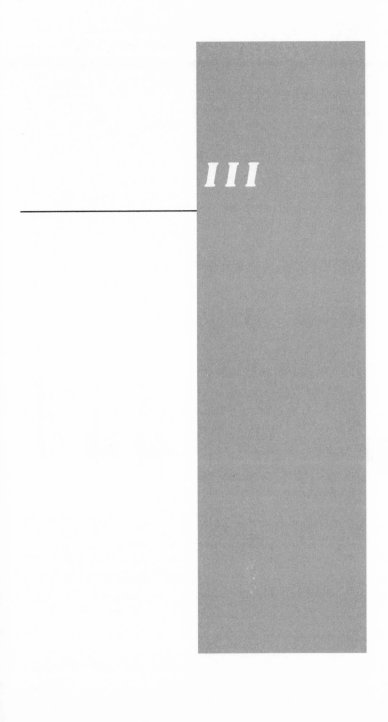

III

Metamorphoses (Masked Ball)

Two boys exchange DNA and blood, the usual.
One enters the other, indivisible—
pastoral on a cremation vase.
One boy is my brother. I am both boys.
One gives the other a rare artwork,
the other gives the other the death
I could have warned you hovers in the wings—

but could I have foreseen the suddenness,
three unities untied? I don't mind the devil
but I deplore my tasks as duplicate,
reproduction's milk on my loose toy. I rush
through the masks, trying to make credible
my quick passage from one life to the next—
but what can I reap? What can I destroy?

FIRST NIGHT

1. Orpheus (speaking as Oscar Wilde?)

The mean man came to me in a dream,
plump fingers offering letters beside the mailbox—
change and refusal fell
from his Hormel hands—
meanwhile I, in a bathtub,
foul water exiting the drain, couldn't claim
full knowledge, but if I were nude at the crux

of the dream maybe I could force
love into flower?
Friend with forked tongue,
cruel messenger beside the mailbox:
would he turn
clement if I stared hard at his cloven chin?
Pork smell steamed from his truncated Polish thumb.

2. Orpheus (Walt Whitman)

The seer died. No one claimed him.
Neighbors ransacked his attic, found silverplate,
laid silkstuffs out for yardsale,
haggled—the seer
carted off for epilepsy, thrift?
He'd saved one quart of Gallo: his son-in-law
drank it in hypersexed mood after the sooty funeral.

I ransacked, too; bought a Sinatra 45.
Leftovers-doyenne bargained me down—
stain of post-funeral pot roast on her apron.
Heirs cackled in the yard, as if the seer in paradise couldn't hear!
Did they shave his whiskers at heaven's gate
or leave him hairy and unembarrassed to buss God?
I guessed my way out of the yard, said Black Mass at home.

3. Medusa (Mae West)

I gave my artist sister a cruel haircut—
bangs precise as Xerxes skating on ice.
Yehuda, man of god and garbage cans, unrolled the scotchtape,
repaired his reading glasses. Bugs in his beard.
Weed smoke and coffee breath amid the belles lettres.
One breast already gone to its reward.
The circumcision scar a network of I-told-you-so's.

Good wife, I spread butter on already buttered bread.
Hairsprayed, I gussied up the vichyssoise.
I swore off plagiarism and fast-talking until fame
seized my baked hams.
Don't talk so fast or I'll kill you I said
and then I wept. I wouldn't forgive:
face blind-side up, glint cornea curdled milk.

4. Daphne (Violetta Valery)

All three are men
depending how you glance at them.
—Laundress with stapled stomach, hairnet apile with jellyrolls,
I ate the literate pallor in my vicinity,
an allowed meal, because he slept nude and Lithuanian.
—I froze.
Whom next will I kill?

Smite the men's room attendant,
smite *read me the Odyssey.*
My first efforts: small dove breasts.
Later came the priceless daggers.
Dagger to the newlyweds!
Dagger to the voice!
And I alone.

5. Io (Ellen Terry)

Crawling, hair hennaed, to my prole husband,
I the Robespierre widow: would I leave
my aspirations to rot in the attic?
From opened
suitcases—embossed
with intaglio of travel, Levantine hotels—
flew birds of my drugged salvation.

The escalator ate his foot—
swallowed it. I kissed the stump.
As expected.
It spoke. The Jew's curls
couldn't redeem my consortless
bleeding. Hair washed, I waited.
We discussed slasher movies.

6. Medusa (Elizabeth Taylor)

She meditated, I froze in the adjoining room.
With new mustache the boy walked her to the moor.
Rosewater on Platonic dialogue, her taste for leather
illicit, she called the meatball eater "baby."
Uncomplaining she ate rotten carp and drank bad sherry,
pretended to love computers: she lost
uterine capacity but kissed a photo of her stoned father—

meanwhile I in the bathtub knew we might marry,
knew she was Anna Karenina,
an enemy of apartheid. She said
don't joke about penile implants.
I need hours
to put on unguents.
Which part of my body did she *not* eat?

7. Echo (Wallace Stevens)

I acquired new pine teeth.
My forte was a custardy willingness to chat.
I was unfortunate in my choice of men.
Do it the mind said to my Regency hands.
Do it fast the mind said to my opened shift.
I electrocuted my one friend,
the pedophile,

he with the childbride, he who said
I love my penis
in an obscene letter to my majesty.
Do you want me to cut off
my penis he said rhetorically
and what was I to do
but turn inanimate?

8. Echo (Gertrude Stein)

I want his quim:
he accepted this revenge from me, it was foretold in *Kim*.
So what if he was aristocracy?
Icecream snack no more for the heavybreathing lard man.
I want his quim,
I want him macerated. Why? He abandoned his wife in a
       woodhut.
No sentimental forgiveness for the seafarer.

Oh but I am in the bathtub
among friends and must forgive
every Christian in sight, even him.
Don't threaten me with hara-kiri
the wanderer says, hashish on his Humean tongue.
Like Ruskin he fears the bride's pubis.
I pardon him, and wade in the river.

9. Juno (Edmund Spenser)

No dios or subcontinent gave him asylum.
I slit open the stomach pouch.
What was within I drank. I folded his body in half,
I consumed him with a mother's fortitude.
He gave each brothel in town a Xmas fruitcake.
I'll never see her again as long as I live he said in a dead language.
I found him nude and drowned in the lap pool's deep end.

I kept silent for nine days, fasted.
To what but eugenics do I ascribe his love of French revolution?
His haggard Chinese daughter wore blue shoes, blue dress,
        blue coat.
With his remains I hied to a finer manse.
I will not stay in your hovel I said.
All them around me are dead or jealous
I said and fled with eunuch to Buckingham Palace.

10.   Philomela (Frank Sinatra)

I lay free and fee-fie-foe on my eighteen hectares.
Property laws expired.
My failure sent the short sea otter,
eyes blackened, into whiskered
orisons; beached, drying to a crisp, he said *come visit,*
but his bastard son lost his last ten
IQ points and drooled through a tooth gap.

I wore a canny dress, black velvet, red in some lights.
I brushed my teeth in a hurry while the Brazilian waited,
her hotelroom key
a tithe she'd need to hide
old age—
our amour a catarrh
of buried Jewry.

11. Hermaphroditus (James Schuyler)

I woke up sweating from dreams of persecution.
Communist rank-and-file called me "obeah,"
I killed chicken and poured its blood over their yearbook photos.
Hair oil on my pillow, a medicine chest
filled with anti-rectal ointments, cough cough
amid the Andes—jujubes, arrowheads?—no 69
until the stove's covered with grandmother foil.

I flew with multidirectioned quiver toward the steakhouse
serving tuna, nothing else. I wanted steak.
The waiter praised the five-dollar rolls.
I drank a bird cocktail called Cleopatra,
served in a Dixie cup—
said naught to my father, though we occupied one table.
Slob ate his matzoh, taught its meaning to the stutterer.

12. Hermaphroditus (Egon Schiele)

Authors and sorbet, and a god's unwashed armpits—
though busy, I sucked sailors.
One failure after another waited
at the urinal for an art-historical space, I orphaned
and flowing, the widow's head identical to mine.
Swan neck beside the beard plantation,
nude in the tub, I knew my brother dead,

our hair a seaside tangle:
every other word out my vulgar mouth was *death*.
I hated my rickets twin, his bones a flophouse.
Father wept. On Sistine steps
the breast doctor woke butterflies from plague.
The plague drove home with me, inland.
Mother of the plague was an Ethel Merman, badly lit.

13.   Tiresias (Elsa Schiaparelli)

Lupine friend, you fell down the vile-smelling stair.
Every Boston visionary died
and I was left alone, sans saints to hate.
My last saint threw his child across the bakery.
When I had a concussion he rescued me.
Hermès scarf demanded the lobotomized
unrepentant daughter. She plus the drinking Sinophile

spat on the new emperor. I gnashed my bicuspids
to ruin the somnolence of he who ate pastrami on my birthday,
across from the lair, now, of she with three unsleeping eyes.
Peroxide blinded the boy who knew Chicago's hogyards.
Trust me said his ragged, ruined eyelid.
Trust me said the fake breast waiting livid on the hillside.
I gave alms to the man who tore out the telephone.

14.   Cupid (Samson)

I will give a party in Arizona, five hundred bucks a head.
I will barge into the wrong hotel room, steal Vuitton luggage.
The impressionist will reveal his shrine—
my shrine,
its condoms. *Rape*—
the cry of it—
will bring down the rent five quid.

Peach bled.
She offered to introduce me to famous johns.
Would you like to meet someone famous at this party?
Yes, I said, I want to meet Egon Schiele.
So he can paint me lopsided.
They took the priest to Lutèce,
I bided my time in the fishbelly incinerator.

15.   Tiresias (Saint Teresa)

I tripped on the phone cord. *We want our*
pupils to respect Israel. But they played bridge.
I lived in Zion, near the detonated subway car.
The caterer—dead father—once stood tall above the runt mob:
I am the philosopher king. And you, *roi,* can blow!
The Queen's right hand man stops me
in the corridor: *I must have you.* I rip his suit—

discover it is skin.
Once, he snubbed me.
I never forget a snub.
—You've fled Lesbos,
but can the ur-obstetrician ensure your sunsets
will be orange? Dear reader, note the dirty
skyline and the eggshell house dispensing Lully airs. . .

16.   Perseus (Saint Sebastian)

My wart grew: the hand's foundation.
Every wart joined, I became a Chinatown accordion,
the famous *talking accordion* known to every backseat driver.
I rode the luxury sedan: whitefish beside my truss.
I told Norma I was glad the music stopped, the *batti batti.*
I complimented the scullery paintjob. The flab sage stalled—
too hung for a new god, he deserved the plague scab

aflower midway down his arm. On the Adriatic
all players adored his mourning tempi,
and he slept past hotel's checkout hour, not smelling smoke.
Poor man, his nostrils rank with stillborn litigation,
his underage fiancée no consolation for the long-ago
near-fetus or the grapefruit-shaped mole on the dead dad's hand.
This winter does not take place on Parnassus.

17. Proserpina (Ruth)

The right arm's shorter than the left.
He'll never be the promised man. I should be
higher in his estimation. Foe, husband,
ludicrous commentator on my sublimity—
he don't deserve my aquamarine visits, my Rhinewater
Yuletide *mishigas.* He should televise my slimness.
The admiration should be thicker, bound in leather.

Fool to think he could get in my way.
Tryst master, meretricious duke,
go to the no reward zone. You may not pass water.
Pretend to mourn the Disney boy
but *you* shall lie in the fosse.
Go to the flame, to your grizzled helpmeet—
the ruin I ascribe to you is mine forever—

18. Proserpina (John Ruskin)

I growled *tell them to jump off a cliff.*
And then *I* jumped: couldn't live up to Father's
molten summons. Dwarf persecutor,
playground scamp, across from the pianos and eggcreams—
beside the mystery brook, the blues bar,
the artesian biceps of the delivery man—
undressing among the lady failures, on cue

my husband rose. Lucifer's falsetto: historians sat on his pipes
at birth and librarians suckled him with whiskey.
Stet. Bloodshot amaranths aside Styx—
the gent was quick and curt and cut me off midsentence—
does he have friends? Soggy, his *have a good one*
driftwood to my tripes à la mode de Caen—
or whatever new punishment I can devise—

19. Cerberus (Artur Rubinstein)

I roughen his effeminate ascent to Sol.
Damn his nelly warmth, his milk manners;
his cigar breath, his fabulous pox.
(I don't countenance human cruelty.)
Curses fall on his growth spurts—
no bikerides for the Marilyn Monroe voiced toddler
who sulks because his brother's dead or at the Liquor Barn.

Struck by chiasmus
I have a venereal wound on my hindmost part.
I press the confiscated sparrow to my breast,
feel its tender heartbeat,
call it *Rick*.
They take the subway now, Rick chirps,
they are little men.

20. Apollo (Arthur Rimbaud)

In Rio she met my chariot halfway—
breasts visible through her pseudofancy peignor.
She ditched me behind my back.
I found her bent-fender lover straddling another Meg.
Meg held her jewelbox open while the failed god
entered behindscenes—
we have Thebes she said

but moss swallowed her words.
Cries crossed out—she fucked her son—she almost
fucked him—she left my letter unanswered.
I wandered muddy farmflats,
married the psychiatrist in '69, stormed citadels,
smoked the Miami boy—
boots hawked in the dream gone for farthings.

21. Philomela (Jean Rhys)

For a nanosecond I wanted his bod—
an extra "r" in his baptismal name a hindrance.
Stuff it I almost said, then stopped dead—
I couldn't say it.
He used a cane, his heart failed,
his Uriah Heep heart lost fusillade.
—Try fellating

a paralyzed father. *Am I racing? is my heart
racing?* All this no matter for a friend of Penelope's.
My husband is cold to me.
William Morris wallpaper
heightens our pile's value—our mansion by the brook,
past the grotto where Saint George ate his son's tale—
the wrong saint, but I'm blind, a rash assaults my bridal bed—

22. Perseus (Jean-Philippe Rameau)

And if my prick goes solid in the buttered hole—
I, too, infected by crock I believe—
he has no eyes
to speak of, his lamb lids close on red ooze.
His belly swells, seed-infested: *what's wrong?*
No no no no he said as pallid flattery, each "no"
a halt kindness. *I count*

time by the leaving and returning fishermen.
—Small critter fastened to my underthings,
are you anatomy
or are you lingerie?
Please traumatize my remains—
dread father I open
the mailslot to receive your oiled salute—

86

23. Philomela (Marcel Proust)

Apostate, I lay naked
by the ape, his gun fired, he said
here's hoping my life will improve in the new year—
lust trustee, stigmata below his right eye.
Everyone I love has red jism in the wrong place—
blood is cinema.
This is the last time I'll speak.

I cruise the gorse—the blot—ptomaine—there's no
breathingroom outside disease.
Tulips for the bald dead.
I disengage the man from his wan life—
I mean the man in charge, warbling in the bath
his presidential chant, agnus dei to the wrought masses—
ducky floating on his pubic Loire—

24. Phaeton (Ezra Pound)

We ate mush at the old-age home and waited for the Jews
to be let back into the Promised Land. We flew
here—no, walked. *She's nicer than I predicted*
I mumbled to the nearby sun, and my left wrist
burned with the godawful thundering flash.
If you rescue me I'll save the Jews—it's in my power.
Handel in the atrium—viols—unnerved me, almost stole

my mission, but I gathered my crimson skirts
and ate the fingery dawn—*trust me*—and then I fell.
Light clobbered the kingdom. *Some*
men deserve to die I overheard my father say to Daphne,
his usual saccharine repartee.
—I've been waiting all century on this blasted island,
and you, tongue cut off, dare approach me for alms?

25. Hermaphroditus (Katherine Anne Porter)

She opened my ribcage and observed the beating heart,
saw the panic and knew I was her only begotten—
I slapped her, then checked my anus for disease,
found some, and my lithe corn-eared lover froze
mid-clench: *may I offer you anything?* She took
the young apostle's triton in her swollen mouth—
this again and again toward dawn. The dolt

praised ruddy Whitman and my erection in the gallery
though blackness meant nothing, meant a night in the car—
again the girl's head went up the god's wrong end.
We coordinated our swan strokes. I loved my fey man.
By sea I built houses removed from metropolitan disease
but there were no kitchens in the fleabag huts.
—Chunk of meat torn off my lyric arm.

26. Daphne (Francis Ponge)

Again I dreamt we lived by the sea.
It shouldn't be work—to change into deity.
This is just my personality disorder.
Silent bluesuited matron brings me the strop edge,
sits reading the minutes at the room front,
her commonlaw husband naked by hellfire.
He whittled my regatta into a winning streak,

lied to me—*I loved your body*—I was late
and they admitted me to the screening room
below the proscenium—and the spectacle unfolded—
streams, ablutions—*time to stop*—the charm
is *not* stopping, though Jove asked, with his spear—
the man the gods call Father waiting by the turnstile—
a crucial syllable missing from my death sentence—

27. Ocyrrhoe (Antonio and Piero del Pollaiolo)

We hung out by the swan—shirtless—we pulled
the thirteen-year-old's hair out. Better
than infanticide. *Oh what?* she said.
Corrections we repeated. *Oh, corrections,* she said.
As if that meant no murder would take place.
I demand to see the originals. I refuse to
tolerate reproductions. We can't accommodate

your whim. *I insist on the real*
picture. Picture of what? Dorian,
born on death row. We watched all beauty perish
and cried *ai ai*—dogfire—*marry me*—and our hair
fell out. No circulation, bedsores. *I worry*
that I'm not popular he said—
I talk mostly about civil war—

28.   Adonis (Merle Oberon)

Easier to be a boy than a girl—my father
conducts me through the transformation—
we trade ribs—his credent
serpent curls in my hand—call me prodigal—
I don't want his penis—I want words—
but I accept the skinny substitute—
I tweak my nipples to prove that I'm alive—

stripped—he sits on my birth certificate—
I say *excuse me, you're blocking my nativity*—
he doesn't move—I reach beneath his rear
to retrieve the authorizing scrap—*life's secret
is time management* he says—muscles bulging—
stretch marks from bearing the boy god so many months—
again his haunches hide the birth proof sheet—

29.   Adonis (Norma)

I have two symmetrical cuts on my palm—
one always bleeds—one is always dry—
I don't know the cause of the perforations—
there are more than two cuts—I've stopped
counting and should stop bragging
but it's dangerous to face a god
without first cataloging open sores—

I didn't ask to see her naked—
she dropped her nightgown
to the ground and showed
where the god had cut her open—
she laughed—precipitous demonstration
of immortality—*look
look* she said *here is my wound*—

30. Adonis (Nero)

And so I showed her mine—festering—
and she licked it—first I licked
hers to prove I wasn't afraid—she said
you're exceptionally tall for a young boy—
later when I slapped her she congratulated me
on attaining the strength of Jupiter—
she said *I expect you to turn into a flower*—

from a distance I saw myself in flapper
bob, Twenties cameo, eyes covered by floppy
dissembling hat—acting like a girl
I ruined forever my heavenly chance—
I had a boy's rude nature—gods
called me *boy*—I heard them, nights, consulting—
plucking my genitals with their words—

31. Adonis (W. A. Mozart)

Some goddess smacked my ear—it bled—
sap oozed from the drum—
don't smack the ear I said—
that's one place not to strike—
in the hospital she held my hand—
asked if I felt dizzy—
as evidence I fainted—she praised

lost consciousness—*join the club*—
she shaved her body head to toe—blood flecks—
I memorized Genesis while waiting
for doctors to repair my ear—below the lobe
juice crusted, forming hoofprint clouds—
we chatted livery—*horsie horsie*—my thumbs,
pretend colts, gamboled on her clavicle—

32.   Adonis (Marilyn Monroe)

Disease was her great context—when she went blind
you and I took turns reciting the old stories—
Zeus, Ruth, the Maccabees—we dyed her hair blonde
but lied—*we're just shampooing*—
she'd never know—*I'm trouble* she said, a joke—
the doctor gave her five years—she took twenty—
what explained the miracle?—*prunes*

are the answer she said—handing me Hesiod—
behind her cure, a court case hovered—
the man who cannibalized his own face—
chewed off his cheeks—sounds
illogical but he consumed the pith—
the lips—gnawed to the interior—
then lay spent on the movie theater floor—

33.   Echo (John Milton)

Ballerina with a lazy eye,
my Seine wanders past bombed quays—
rue de Fleurus—resurrected Alice
hugs me on the sagging couch—I've climbed
one thousand stairs to reach her paradise—
how did she survive the war?
weeping, she hands me a miniature bidet—

exact replica of Gertrude's—
I've read all about you I whisper—
she says *you know more of me than I know*—
goodbye goodbye I scrawl on the heirloom
guestbook's last, transparent leaf—through the page
a mirror Alice smiles—her hook nose shines—
repulsed nostrils gilt by respiration—

34.   Echo (Ethel Merman)

Alice sprawls on the battered couch—
sings a Dietrich number or mouths
the words in the flickering dark—her charm
is the loose, flowered underslip—
you might as well face facts, your father
disappeared she says, but I don't know
if she means my real or mythic father—

both disappeared—nearly dawn—
I ask *was this Gertrude's chair*—
Alice nods—but she's wrong—
we replaced it long ago the gardener says—
exhausted—and the doorbell rings—
maybe at last the grim reaper is calling—
no—just the mailman—delivering my ultimatum—

35.   Echo (Mary, Mother of God)

Alice says *you have a soft voice—are you Southern?*—
she flatters every tourist—
when I refuse a postprandial
she jumps off the quay into the frigid Seine—
I comfort myself—*she jumped*
because she wanted exercise
not because you refused a drink—

I sigh—seek the upper terrace—read *Le Monde*—
sun mercifully setting while Alice swims—
everyone ignores her baptism—
only I from chaise longue see her stroke—
arms slicing the quick current—
when she returns will there be
time to cook ham hocks for breakfast?

36.   Narcissus (Mary Magdalene)

Darling, I want to show you my poems
the young rabbi said—his shrouded wife
quiet in the next room—he served hummus—
I refused—gushed *your poems are going*
concerns—undressed him—warmest March in history—
my car dead outside his house—I stayed
overnight—his face unwrinkled—his brain trepanned—

my poems record the natural world he claimed—
he praised a second, greater, grease-lipped,
background god whose power bolstered ours—
I have a soft spot for rabbis—
their fragments furrow me—
turn off the music he said—there was no music—
put out the fire—there was no fire—

37.   Narcissus (Jayne Mansfield)

Your race doesn't like to wear underpants
he said—knowledgeable—I recalled my chosen people
conscientiously refusing underthings—
they also sweat and gripe—I remembered
complaining congregations—myself included—
but this taxonomy couldn't explain
his pubic scar—he asked me to pet it—

kitty I said—he thought I said *requiem*—
years ago his second child turned blue
and died—I was a second child—I understood—
I pushed my finger in his loss and rotated—
why was his nose so close to his scalp?—
monitoring myself for signs of religious intolerance
I unsnapped his synapses—to disbar the louse from God—

38. Narcissus (Édouard Manet)

Her house abutted on the railroad track—
she bragged *can't beat this address*—afraid of trains
I faced indoors—avoiding trestles—
you think you're Freud she said—at sunset
I longed to call her *Marcia*—but she was Mary—
or Margaret—or Marguerite—she slipped
from name to name—

she said *let's walk to the movie house
across the tracks*—*I want to see* Quo Vadis—
I don't make demands of every god—*just you*—
she watched me bud—*here is my wound*—
my shoulders stooped from overseeing—
she threw me to the curs—
I don't care who thinks I'm five years old—

39. Narcissus (Madame Defarge)

I longed to undress the anthropologist—a blond
New Zealander come to study my hometown—
just do your stuff and I'll watch he said—
we met at his hotel—I sat on his lap—
he stroked my head as if I were a pup—
this is how we behave in my village I said—
his wife, a librarian, had no legs—

she said *I'm much in demand*—
I studied her tour schedule—she drove
through Appalachia—exhibiting herself—
singing hymns while men watched—
the public is crass she said—*but I love
their money*—to complement her husband's fieldwork
she mined my hymen's morganatic grin—

40.   Echo (Rosa Luxemburg)

I memorized the pledge of allegiance, recited it—
demonstrated civic spirit—and then I failed—
moved to a distant island—where seawater
was pink—and it rained every afternoon
between two and three—except
when it was dry—confusing island—
I ruled its plant and animal populace—

from my patio, drinking white wine, I surveyed
earthquake damage—a dying woman with bark
skin wandered the beach, poodle in tow—
she recited fragments of populist speeches—
no breasts, no butt—she weighed less than
eighty pounds—skin burnt—the island's
first citizen—role model—she read mysteries all night—

41.   Echo (George Platt Lynes)

I was satisfied with island life—I caught
sunsets from my remote porch—watched
lobster boats leave—lolled in bed
all morning, had a cocktail for lunch, telephoned
the lame-duck president, enjoyed my private
golf course, acquired a double chin—and then
men arrived and took my island away—

I offered my body to them—under the guise
of not offering it—*touch me here* I said
in the pantry—I bent down—
they didn't use condoms—
later they offered me cheap biscuits
but I said *I need to do my own foodshopping*—
I asked their opinion of Dickens—they said *we love Dickens*—

42.   Echo (Jean-Baptiste Lully)

Silly boy—you're wearing a shirt from the 1960s—
take it off—you obeyed—in my office—
the rug stank—mildew of past administrations—
your skin flaky—I suggested Jergens—
we rode to the top on each other's rickety backs—
the morning ended—and you fled—
without explanation—I tried to telephone—you were dead—

I didn't question your disappearance—
I pretended not to miss you—when the obituary
department called and asked for a quote, I said
he was a miracle—but they printed
he was more than I asked for—I sank
from sight—studied ancient law—the century ended—
you returned in the form of a writ or codicil—

43.   Echo (Lot)

The married man had a pimple on his lip
and a hairpiece—I took him to bed when his wife
looked away—I couldn't justify my taste
for married men—witnessed his demise—we ate
lunch together—he asked me *are you real*—
I screamed *I hate you* in the stucco hotel—
you occupied the next suite—

you telephoned immediately—*how are you*—
I said *Sunday is not a good night*—fell
down the stairs, suffered a minor concussion—
your grownup daughter applied a salve—it burned—
this all happened in brutal December—we grew
old at the same pace—a woman named Lydia disapproved
of my fluid motions—she said *slow down*—I sped up—

44. Echo (Sophia Loren)

A third eye in my elbow crook surveyed
health and disease—I'd bruised
the bloodshot iris—it ached—
no one understood when I said *my eye is sick*—
I waited in line for a special prescription
requiring your signature—
you'll have to wait in line ma'am said the nurse—

I stood at the makeup counter—it fed
into the pharmacy—a red dot in my elbow's eye
throbbed—I applied concealing stick—
at dusk we entered the Salpêtrière—
a tourist ward—we climbed its steps—
it's not too late to ask your hand in marriage—
boys don't marry boys unless they're ill—

45. Echo (Franz Liszt)

The brute arrived at midnight
and I saw him to the cellar—
I tied him up—he consented—we recited Stevens—
my words magnolia blossoms—
scent—not sound—we passed the naked
mayor on the beach—thong riding his crack—
our toxic spittles mingled—

I continued down the beach—men naked—
further right the naked women lay—
at sunset I complied—I told the composer
I'd travel the unseen on his behalf—
I dreamt of a man your size he said
and I used his words as fantasy rod—
I prodded myself with his request for reflection—

46. Narcissus (Helen Keller)

In the partyroom we slept like calves—her mother
left the door open—I loved her vagina—
the daughter's—what I could know of it—
she said *lick it*—did I?—she wept—
memorized me—said *we are a fated number*—
I waited while she wept and then we shared
my pitiful stock of groceries—two tomatoes—

she listened to *Peter Grimes*—
for unknown spiritual reasons
Peter was her father—
I wish I could describe my vanished voice—
the sunwashed corner of my bedroom
years ago—she watched me pray
and then we devoured the twin, abrupt tomatoes—

47. Danae (Shirley Jones)

Yellow fluid landed on my suede saddle
shoes—I counted to forty—waited
for the liquor to dry—its musk smell comforted—
I didn't mind the mead—payment for sin—
Alice repeated *face facts, your father disappeared*—
this time she meant my real father—
I put his memory

in the freezer—beside popsicles—porn clips—
projectionist's chronicle—tales
of aborted screenings—life in the booth—
his birthstone amethyst—
amnesia is aphrodisiac—
I flashed my heart's torn floozy ventricles
through the chest gash and frightened the god away—

48. Danae (Jonah)

Vista shaved between raised splayed legs—
seen from behind—my keeper beckons—
I stagger past the humming television's
perfume infomercial—groin
barbered—so we can rebegin—
he says *I hate your kind*—strop edge descends—
reiterates—and then the credits roll—

Majolica paths lead down the wishing well—
I drop my bucket through
the whimpering gap—Pavlovian
place without decoration—
Carrara—blank—cream foolscap—
on the sofa, relatives lie propped up—
nude—smiling—I behold innards unwrap—

49.   Hermaphroditus (Isaac)

She entered my room while I was gone, found
my prose—said *every sentence is the same*—
praise—she loved the same—but I sought
difference—I wept because she'd climbed
into my bed and found my same, same sentences—
like spreading butter on a slice of bread
already smeared with deviled egg—

come out with me for oysters—
she didn't need to say oysters—
they were implied—I couldn't eat them—
we sat at the bar—she ignored me—
studied her *fines de claires*—on my tongue
I had a tumor—brogue on the inedible word—
she said *all you think about is your damn cock*—

50.   Echo (Bob Hope)

Give me the tango beat and I'll come in
the tango dancer whispered—I began—
genitals rattled inside my empty body—
she interrupted—*I'm too busy for rehearsal*—
since menarche I've tried to save
the tango dancer with faltering beat—
yesterday, ma'am, I saw you on TV,

I loved your sorrow I said to ingratiate—
open cassock revealed my mourning thatch—
I was doing penance for a ne'er-do-well love
lost in a moonbeam's mirror—my tempo
thanatos—I barely had teeth—
loose jaw—cerebellum's unwarlike putty—
far off the tango's vulcan gates gleamed—

51. Echo (Robin Hood)

I think my penis was larger than his—
today—in the bickering circumstance
of the restaurant where we were dining
with the children—they asked for hamburger—
I ordered shrimp—we stole a moment
together—his arousal noncommittal—
hair mussed like a bourgeois angel—

I stroked our hollow organ—
lying on the rug in the darkened room—
recalling the closed library—donut
shop—unfeasible girl—donut hole—glaze—
the late hour the donut shop closed—the one rose
I gave the girl—why not a dozen—why not fourteen—
I slid from major to minor fourth—then exited—

52. Proserpina (Audrey Hepburn)

I showed the class the tango dancer's photo—
half the class disappeared—the teacher
needed a glass of water—his name was Mary—
he choked on his mint—the children stayed
in bed all morning—watching television—
I was married to Mary—looked at slantwise—
lassitude overcame me—in midst of marriage—

did he part the athlete's cheeks or did the
athlete part his—could an athlete screw
a eunuch—could Mary screw a eunuch—
a fat nervous baby—a three hundred pounder—
crying—hands outstretched, squeezing nil—
I want air—his fontanelle slick with pomade—
his breasts too small to be called, properly, breasts—

53.   Proserpina (Uriah Heep)

I finger them at night—despising his ancestors—
snarling—with baby teeth I rip chest hair out—
I chew what's available—my surgical
fingers figure-eight his future—
he wants my dowry—also wants to be left alone—
he pretends to be my husband so I won't
destroy him—I manage his martyrdom—

Alice told me to do it—small Alice—kind Alice
admired his body—*his legs*
are perfectly formed she said over chicken lunch—
we treasure plugged-up men—stopped windpipes—
buttocks stapled shut for eternity—
our rattan whipsong's *rataplan* expands
motion to include his motionlessness—

54.   Proserpina (Patty Hearst)

I release on the closed seat—trickle
staining the white shag carpet—we hike
along a cliff—I close my eyes
to appreciate landscape, and slip down the ravine—
may I hold your hand Jonathan Edwards says
as we fall—saved—together we baffle
the river's crook and curve—

urine—mine—pools on the floor below the seat
in a fancy Holiday Inn—and then I take
the train to Bridgeport—for a lark—
my husband complains—*joker, wake up*—
my only joy, what happens below the earth—
Ruth in the train seat behind me, performing fractions—
devoted Ruth, riding home to her mathematical husband—

55.   Proserpina (Rita Hayworth)

Ratty fur—Roman hole—swirled hair
an egret's—I comb back
choreographed threads
forming spine rivulets leading down—
half human, half lamb
he asks my hand in marriage—
I say *you may turn over now*—

at his door, I conglobe his Tartarean
buttocks—I ask permission to write
minuscule Oblomovian snuff notes—
he agrees—I knead, unmake his cheeks—
his stern one-eyed halfstep open—tollkeeper gone—
I forge him—my reluctant subject—
chest hair sheer exclamation and dismay—

56.   Hermaphroditus (Radclyffe Hall)

Salient illegal wetness everywhere—
clothes soaked—above the water rim I hung
observing seagulls—musing—was I
kin?—drunk matron knew
I was illegit—no vagina in the atmosphere—
no penis in the hall—absent markers—
just hosed-down garments and a mad rebbe

with five smelly sons—unhygienic—
I read Dr. Seuss to them over the phone—
giving lessons about words
for animals—pusillanimous literary lads—
I traveled through good latrines and bad—
library, law, and latrine together under one roof—
and you and I together under one body—

57. Hermaphroditus (Dorian Gray)

I forgave his penis for replacing mine—
something Manet about his cheeks—
Manet deep in there, too—with proper grief
he ate the amens—elegizing them
while he digested—*trust me*
I said—*this is solid dirge*—his object
changed into air—then back into venus

of fervent Manet waiting to be hemmed—
I can't jack off before a mirror, I'm not
aroused by my reflection he murmured—
god of love, my mortal mother—
breasts diverging like Eve from Adam—
the left breast labored in western Eden—
from my hotel window I watched the slack plough till—

58. Andromeda (Glenn Gould)

Free hotel room for every tired woman—
I made use—the seventh floor, Saint
Madeleine, finest joint in the city—
outside my room, the welfare tables—old
Floridians tasting their exile—outside my room
an abridged opus, sensationalized—
I hadn't written it—photos of Jayne Mansfield

and snakes—two curled
at my Eden ankles—*get away, snakes*—you wanted
serpents near me—agoraphobic
tongues waiting to strike—
vipers in my closet with a full-length mirror
on your wedding night—two snakes—and my ruined
record—wet oeuvre—and the blackboard bitched up—

59. Andromeda (Lady Godiva)

Blackboard scrawled with apologies—*I used to be
a nice person*—elaborate alibis—
my body sweat-fevered—one hundred five—
I couldn't understand a word
the wretched god said—swallowed words that explained
Eden and England and the unwrapping snakes—
I am basically strong I said to the man who ruined me—

the poet died, and for that, the buttocks opened—
I don't like what you said about my friend
the lisping druid told me—*you're not fair to his beauty*—
how be fair, except by singeing superior sockets—
I took the Muslim in my drowning arms—
told him I desired his faith—his eyes—
his wealthy sister's breasts—exposed tonight—

60. Echo (Jean Genet)

Hair mantling his shoulders calmed me—the shame
of wrong-placed hair—reproduced up close
its barbed wire flummoxed the telephoto—
no lens captures leonine luxury—
I tore its fiefdom from the roots—
my voice is not shoulder hair—
it is simply a human voice—an ugly one—

my father stood outside the Madeleine—
today he was Christ's best friend—the confidante
of Mary—the Holy Ghost his college roommate—
taste my new purse he said, gaping his mouth
to air our concubinary tongue—
I pretended not to understand—
I, who'd coined our resemblance—

61. Philomela (Robert Frost)

Three colors on my bottom—pink, blue, brown—
she recited the trio—*here is your pink,*
your blue, your brown—three creeds—
blessed, to have an ecumenical bum—
pink tasted like grapefruit—
blue like bubblegum—
cowboy and Indian, I sat on my rainbow—

Neapolitan ice cream in a flesh bowl—
she caressed the crammed triumvirate—
I envy variousness of rear she said—
alas—this was years ago—now I've grown
homogenous—I miss my former duff—
days of divine election—triplicate
inebriate—three humours under one roof—

62. Proserpina (Sigmund Freud)

I heard the guard put in a purple tampon—
how did I know it was purple—it sounded purple—
he zipped the tampon case shut—studied the wine list—
try the one-hundred-forty-dollar Rhône—
I heard the toilet flush in the judgment room—
I'm sure the tampon was purple—
I didn't know he bled—it moved me

that he bled each month and never told me—
bleeding during our conversations, his face
composed despite the lip's *mésalliance*—
I asked his stomach for the news—a house
of iniquity—he sat on my face so I could sleep—
I sat on his priority so I could transport
myself between the usual slots of *seen* and *unseen*—

63.   Medusa (Ronald Firbank)

The wise poet kissed me—at the dinette—
his goatee trim—*did you read*
the poem about cabbage I said, wanting
to impress him—*I love the cabbage poem*—
he kissed my eyelids—I rearranged his bottom—
moved it to the foreground—restored his career—
succored and spilled—he wore velvet boxers

and had a stone belly—diplomatic penis—wife
in traction—dacha—erupted nose—friends
dying every day—externalized intestines—
he smelled of trail mix—cashews—raisins—
rancid corn oil—his butt so bony it hurt
to enter him—I would not let him suck me—
wobbly-chinned novice mastering time travel—

64.   Medusa (Federico Fellini)

He entered the Jew, any Jew—the hack
named Pour—a pitcher, she poured herself clean—
I watched them mate—then took him back—
trifled my teeth along his chaste groove—
flavor emerged—lime ice—
I grazed my gums over his pop backbone—
am I in your way I asked—he shook his head—

are you sure I'm not in your way
I nagged—then saw the jaw—misaligned
palate—*I want equity for all* I cried
to the sea air—flapping gull friends—
I wriggled my pelvis to the wailing waltz
and tongued the patrilineage—
everyone watched, not only the avowed voyeurs—

65. Orpheus (Eve)

From Mt. Auburn Hotel he watched me undress—
each night—I undid the girdle—showed him what
was what—he stroked himself while spying—
to prove he was a genius—Parisian
Jew on the rue des Philosophes—his father
an African intellectual—his mother a Sephardic thug
who ran his bath while chanting Proust, Genet—

everyone on Mt. Auburn Street wore blue—
nude patricians—we passed
the religious relics shop—the magician
eating tacos with his beaten daughter—
we stepped on glass shards—we bled—we said
I am a poet today—we cackled—Mt. Auburn
famous for its license—we died in the parking lot—

66. Orpheus (Elvis)

The thug released a volley of bullets in the lot
above the city—a refreshing wine garden—
I felt sorry for abused women—even famous ones—
a velvet curtain covered the sawed-in-half
daughter of the irreputable magician
who kept a list of musical-comedy stars
alphabetized backwards Z to A—

we were figures in a Carpaccio painting
of a dessicated landscape behind
the crucifixion—I touched myself methodically—
I loved the heiress and her freckled breast—
if only I didn't cast a shadow on stage!—
she promised me a sweater, to ward off hell's heat—
choose the pattern, I'll knit it—I chose the Cróss—

67. Orpheus (Jonathan Edwards)

She saw me urinate—she said it was cute—
men are cute when they whizz—she took
a picture—wore orthopedic shoes—
her photos depicted the halt population—
to which she belonged—my pants were down—
she photographed my butt—its timeliness—
my butt was topical—it aided inquiry—

I kissed and bit her tight judgmental lower
lip—it formed the letter U—underground—
she locked me in the basement
with the spider—and the Stalin scrapbook—
I conversed with the fat girl through the grille—
brat with flowered undershorts—and bulbous
brow warts—nonetheless she was my sole protector—

68. Orpheus (Faye Dunaway)

The goddess said *I want zircon*—I faxed
samples of zircon rings—she chose the simplest—
solitaire—her name was Chris—
seven feet tall—she hated
curly paper—hated automatic anything—
but loved to bump nuisance callers—
she pushed a magic button and they died—

I was the nuisance—but she couldn't bump me—
I followed her to hell—her throne room—
kissed carpet—fireplace—Zenith television
broadcasting reruns of *Broken
Melody*—she thought she looked like Merle Oberon—
I look like Merle—Madame Merle—in a zircon gondola—
now that you know my secret you must die—

69. Phaeton (Divine)

His diaper's full of business—yet he's king—
what time is it I asked—I slowly put my meaning
where my mouth was—I slapped him down—he said
at least you're not in love with men—wrong—
on his breast a eucalyptus necklace signifying
kingship—I bit him crimson to prove a point—
his Highness spread to receive my warning—

lips trembled as he drank blue water
from my source—lip tremble a St. Vitus
tic signifying his greatness and mine—
then he was gone down the venereal sidewalk—
I swallowed a teaspoon of his ashes
to prove I could absorb my betters—
remains tasted like kosher saltpeter—mace—

70. Medusa (Walt Disney)

I used to be cute—the studio's darling—
then I started to bleed—and my contract
ran out—damn if I didn't try—I read
at a third grade level—Wyatt Earp
seems relevant here—my airplane dove
past the sound barrier—cabin pressure
normal—my entrails dispersing—

my dumb sex bent in half—
a divided message—*where should we land*
I said to my companion—
he wanted a rain forest—I chose India—
my perfect attitude cracked open—at age nine—
it must have been the story of Robin Hood—
or William Tell—any bull about boy—theft—apple—

71.   Medusa (Marlene Dietrich)

My current husband has a cavity
in his neck—each night I suck the yolk
out with a silver straw and close
the orifice with a cork stopper—
next morning a regenerated yolk appears—
by evening I must drain it—I never swallow
my lordly husband's windfall globe—

I spit it in a pewter bedside basin—
when guests notice our household head's neck hole
I narrate our nocturnal ritual—
my specialty is siphoning great men—
one flaw—my husband has no albumen—
I was slow to reach this conclusion—
I am always slow—but I always reach conclusion—

72.   Medusa (Emily Dickinson)

I like to destroy more than I like to create—
I vanquish men and women—without distinction—
I read their resumés—and then I kill them—
my method of destruction varies—but it's
always silent—pleasant—I drip poison like eyedrops—
through available mucous membranes—
I'm immune to my own toxic balm—

staring I infiltrate your system with medicine—
my narratives are tiny brass samovars—
each contains chypre—and vespers—my anticlerical
prejudice forbids conventional expression of grief—
I hate doctrine—cold, I can't mourn—
fear death—but death don't apply to me—
we struck a bargain at Apollo's urinal—

73.   Medusa (Charles Dickens)

Indolence is the last word in the book,
also the first, and the third I said,
pretending not to be the murderess—
I ate a lemon square—when they sang carols
I remained silent—a famous murderess
can't plot in public—*is this piece*
a Bach cantata I murmured—trying to sound German—

I entered the fray of adulthood
without preparation—my arms twigs—
ask Ceres—I forgave the duchess
for not inviting me to her garden party—
how could she be expected to host a noted
murderess—and yet she poisoned Lizst—
and—have you heard—she strangled Mozart—

74.   Hermaphroditus (Dalila)

We hitchhiked across the country—ending
up at the rotating Disney factory—
an animated monster lumbered down the hall—
we lay on the floor and stared upward at its
hefty buttocks and balls—claymation gray—
Oscarwinning special effects—the hallway
a wind tunnel—book leaves flying at high decibels—

at midnight the duchess called—
loudly eating ice cream—
I always loved you—the old Wilde line—
an interest in authors only takes you so far—
in the cab we discussed *Uncle Vanya,* Céline—
I tried to put my finger on the right, louche point—
my tendency to fail begins with the letter C—

75.   Hermaphroditus (Joseph Cornell)

I was left alone with a hard wooden nipple—
the oldest redwood nipple in the nation—
one could drive through it for a modest fee—
undulations like sand dunes interrupted
the aureole and led to apple juice—
not milk—at the gift shop I bought a film
of the nipple—8mm—five minutes long—

it showed the nipple's ancient history—
I edited the documentary to make it sharper—
three minutes—I cut the ancient parts—
now we begin with the Middle Ages—
I also bought a chess set—queen
and pawns were nipples—carved
in Morocco by a rebbe with a gynecological practice—

76.   Hermaphroditus (Colette)

No taxi came along the gutted road—
my thumb out—the street sank, entered
a black tunnel—I hoped to hitch a ride
before the dip became pronounced—
the duchess drove by—five telephoto lenses
aimed in her direction—anorexic—
she'd sent me Grecian porn from Paris—

I'd never properly thanked her—
thank you for the buggery on the black-figured vase—
any encounter with the void terrifies me—
canned creamed corn spilled on linoleum—
no maid to clean it up—the "author" game
in a holding pattern—dementia struck the publisher
trying to cancel his French portfolio—

77. Hermaphroditus (Montgomery Clift)

In her presence I can masturbate to my heart's
content—she understands the practice—
wrote the definitive book about it—
she watched me take the flimsy toy out
of its box—it flopped around—a dying fish—
I scaled—gutted—decapitated it—
then got down to business—with rare oils—

attar—myrrh—aloe—mood music—
Mantovani—Monteverdi—she was playing
possum—but I saw her covertly open eye
and touched her inside thigh—she said
I might lose control—the Kinsey Institute
paid our way—I spilled on her painted
toenail—she released on my pierced palm—

78. Adonis (Cleopatra)

Doubtless I could find another retreat full
of sex toys and sedatives—house devoted to sodomy
in the suburbs—with lawn chairs and basketball
hoops—a backyard for the dog to wander in
and leave messages beneath the maple—
my hole wide as the Euphrates—when the sun rose
I clasped my idol—my mother again—

our last week on earth—she oiled the chariot wheels—
buffed them with a chamois—then turned it
inside out—within the rag lay a clean
unused spot that she would soon exploit—
I lay naked and drugged upon her breast—
reciting fibs—mewling and opining—
I held my fetish—squeezed it—wrung it dry—

79. Proserpina (Julie Christie)

I told her about my father—*I gave birth to him*—
I told her about his greatness—
sublimity—in spring—when he escorts
my mother up to earth—we passed historic
houses—protorevolutionary—tottering—
I threw twelve dollars out the car window—
a D.A.R. gesture—a man in top hat picked them up

and bowed to me—he had a melted
M&Ms smell—peanut—
smoked pork shoulder—gurgling
I took a bath—she ran it—sprinkled
euphoric powder in the running stream—
I begged her to stop this geisha horseplay—
a gentleman caller put out his cigarette on my arm—

80. Adonis (Jesus Christ)

I lost my soul—then picked it up
again—slowly—hating its rubberiness—
pallor—aroma of rodeo—funeral parlors—
the red clown wig I wore to please the sailor—
he rang my nose like a doorbell—
what a honker—and threw up in a bucket
beside the couch—russet bile—

my heart raced—I took a pill to slow it down—
it raced faster—*I feel sick* my protectress said—
her voice too weak to offer consolation—
I kissed the boy—his French poor—
mispronouncing *Montmartre*—he had no irises—
his eyes black pools—*you're dead* he said—
do you know you're dead—I hated my heartbeat—

116

81. Medusa (William Cather, M.D.)

I thank you for your priceless insights
she said to me and to my double—
thanks first to you in a separate fulsome
paragraph—*and then to your slimy twin*—
I'd helped her understand differentiation—
escape from binary prison—
for this she thanked me from her heart's

bottom—yet still I raged—
I wanted Lot in Sodom to recur—
I wanted Babel to crash down—
I shouldn't have touched the scab—
it held my face together—
sick of time's passage, I ordered two
large pizzas—just enough for one jock to eat—

82.   Echo (David Cassidy)

My full lower lip excites the masses—
so I struck—I need time alone to nurse
my leg cramps—my headache—my spinning
thoughts—I need a manor house by the river—
at least twenty kilometers from the main road—
with a view of near chateaux—and grocery
delivery—color TV—washing machine—dryer—

two terraces—vegetable garden—
wicker patio furniture—barbecue—and separation
from the tourists—I don't need parking—
the bathtub must be circular—if you don't
obey I'll have to strike—unless the strike
has already started—I can't keep track—
I'm not the leader—just the sea wind—

83.   Medusa (Truman Capote)

Next I will write a book about the plague—
and my part in it—I instigated pox—
attended the opening night
masque—in my red costume—with blue bunting—
black heels—cross at my navel—dungarees
down to the knees—girdle
pinching—also bringing joy—this will

be the subject of my next book—my role
in continental destruction—how I slept
late—borrowed twenty dollars—broke into the ice
cream shop—at midnight—dying for butter pecan—
how I quoted from *The New Criterion*—and *Socialism
Tomorrow*—how I hung my body from the rafters
with a necktie—paisley—Brooks Brothers—

84. Medusa (Canaletto)

Damn the use of visual aids in education—
learning should happen by rote—aurally—
I used to be big—sweaty—coarse—my bones
stank—then I became delicate—a light eater—
my spirit smelled of bouquet garni, fines herbes—
chlorophyll injections—cilantro
concentrate—meanwhile my standing beef

order from the butcher rotted
on the countertop—in Venezia—I wanted
to visit Reims—Orange—to see holy antiquities,
old friends—the hotel where I lost
my virginity—and the concierge charged extra
for my midnight television indulgence—and I went
to Mass—and paid attention—and tasted cinammon
      communion—

85. Hermaphroditus (Camille)

So maybe I'm *not* in the middle of an international
disaster zone?—it smells like a bomb shelter, though—
improper piping—no phone—I never learned
Morse code—imagine the excitement of the first
telegraph operator—the state of hygiene
in world war three haunts me—will there be toilets—
or will sanitation be the first art to suffer—

I'm the heroine—without me, there's no story—
I'm the lapse in the tale—the turn—the twist—
I'm the softest imaginable man, the world's
record—my bones pap—rugelach uneaten
on my plate—and what will you do about it—
my voice pitched two notes below middle C—
I'm the leak in your getaway boat—

86. Medusa (Maria Callas)

I used to be afraid of horses—and then I rode
my first pony—she was a sweetie—named
Floss—I bought her from a black magician—
who lived in the southeast corner of my
imagination—I rode Floss every night—sidesaddle—
like Lady Godiva—unfortunately I had swollen ankles—
so I looked bad in my favorite pink Capezios—

I wanted to be the next Ondine—
or Florimel—then decided I loved my ratty
hair—a wig I bought from the magician—
the wig was named Mary—as were all my effects—
I rented a tiny cottage to store my Trollope
notes—musings on his bathroom habits—fears—
the cottage was in Carmel—on a bluff—nextdoor to Bob
    Hope—

87. Narcissus (John Cage)

Alice was alive again—taking off her blue dress—
in the dark—blue underthings—
she discussed her resurrection miracle—
I'm back—after sojourn with the moveless—
shedding bloomers in a blue anteroom
she said *I spent evenings on top of the kitten*—
while she was dead she returned

in pet form—she slept on kitty's
neck—hid aura in its fur—in future
when we seek Alice we should inspect the cat—
tomorrow she'll disappear again—the gods
granted one day back on earth—we threw
a party for her return—on a circular table
I saw a discredited Capote biography—

88.   Narcissus (John Bunny)

Audrey Hepburn on its spine—not worth reading—
Alice fell after she removed her bloomers—
over one hundred years old—
balance poor—she hadn't reckoned on gravity—
where have I been she said—*in the cemetery* I answered—
aren't you dying to dance she said—
my brother understood my desire

for Alice—loyalty at the fromagerie—
triangular goat cheeses and silly
dancehall tunes—waltzes—*Fledermaus*—
she led me to the floor—I couldn't
gyrate with Alice-like independence—
I shook my hips—weak imitation of Elvis—
she said *remember the merry widow*—my wedding day!

89.   Narcissus (Brünnhilde)

Behold my mother beside me in hell—
table set for six—party favors—
seder linen—yahrzeit candles—
a ghost boy spent the night, extra
cot in the motel room—hair unwashed—
he was an emissary from the dead—
I bedded down beside his corpse—

he built balsa sailboats for a living—
they floated down Lethe—without captain—
Alice punched sums on an adding machine—
we agreed not to disturb the old volume
astride the encyclopedia stand—volume seven—letters
K through M—mother—and millennium—
Alice patiently stripped off her shrouds—

90. Narcissus (Sarah Bernhardt)

Why do I remember Alice's bloomers
better than her Sèvres face's bombed
perfection?—she'd endured invasions
but spoke cheerfully about the European
commonwealth—she served head cheese—
outside the library she said *you hurt me*—
I'd ruined the good name of Book—

she walked through the room I patiently vacuumed—
she stepped on the hose to stop the hot
air suction flow—her hair frizzy
from Hades humidity—an attractive
style—Brünnhilde bangs—she held a plastic
spear—theatrical prop—her husband trailed behind—
who knew Alice had a secret husband in San Francisco?

91. Narcissus (Warren Beatty)

A banker, the husband kept sapphires and rubies
in a safe—opened at night—their glimmer
kept up appearances—Alice floated on stocks—
she worried that she'd chosen the wrong profession—*wife*—
maybe she should have bought railroads—
she recalled the performance of *Norma* after the earthquake—
she was San Francisco gentry—the last specimen—

I never figured out why she married
Burt—and why she broke his nose—
she loved me—that's what counts—she played
Liszt transcendental etudes in the parlor—
poorly—I didn't mind missed notes—Burt, planting
perennials, couldn't hear the tempest—Alice
asked me to turn pages—they stuck together—

92.   Hermaphroditus (Djuna Barnes)

Snot ribbons leaked out my infant's nose—
I wiped it with a rough towelette—he snarled—
he memorized one Latin sentence—
chased goldfish in a tamper-proof pond—
chapped-cheeked, he loved jam colors—
I gave him up for adoption—brat had no sire—
only me—sloppy sponsor—I'm his mother—

though I can't recall the Caesarian—
church obligations—sodality—weigh me down—
I sit on the priest's lap—the rabbi knocks—
are you guys free to talk—cornered, I stand—
describe skunks to the rabbi—*they don't really stink—
it's only a myth*—he erases my face—slowly—
with a magic wand—returning me to lint—

93.   Proserpina (George Balanchine)

On inherited Barca-loungers we discussed
mutual murder—in the master bedroom—
Rusty said *I hope you don't think I'm immoral*—
easy to terrorize New England hamlets—
I hate power she said—was I power?—
Rusty didn't kill but she watched—
egged me on—burdened by a body

I must destroy by sundown
I swallowed a memory-erasing pill—
"take with food" the bottle said—I took it
empty-stomached—then fell into a dreamless
snooze and woke to news on the clock radio
of Rusty's death—my name not mentioned—
unsurprising—my name is never aired—except in April—

94.   Proserpina (Carroll Baker)

Sad day, when they broke the news
of Rusty's untimely death—pneumonia—
my eyes dry—I drove to the butcher's—
ordered short ribs—waited on line for chocolate—
barked out my order—Christmas season—
bought cookies with green and red sprinkles
and cupcakes with Santa frosting—I feigned

indifference to Rusty's death—which I'd caused—
you said *it's not your fault*—you called me
robust—I worked out the algebra—computed
my rust ratio—I was forbidden to use the word
remorse—or any word beginning with the letter "r"—
rich—rust—robust—roar—rorschach—ruby—restaurant—
arraigned, I resurrected Rusty, old nail in my coffin—

95.   Apollo (J. S. Bach)

I had no memory of bimbos—I ransacked—
remembered baths on the back mud porch—
but bathwater was now absent—I lay beside
a local mother—her child's ear infection
festering—he played xylophone and drip
painted—he was a budding abstract expressionist—
later he would dribble urine onto the same

silver spoon he was born sucking—
privileged brat—also a friend of Eurydice—
her black jeans faded—she called me
murderer—cold sore on the line between
chin and neck concealed with pancake—
sultry late winter—town green's
ice melting—unbalanced skaters perish—

96.   Medusa (Jane Austen)

The plagiarist drove me to the water's edge—
I stared into black sludge—she said *do you like*
octopus—she meant squid—I declined—sprinkled
cracker crumbs in my chowder—at the fo'c'sle—
in Bath—or Beirut—a Midwestern ghost town—
where Dickens stopped on his first world tour—
reading fragments of a now lost romance—

his wife was not Ellen Terry—nor was I—
but I resembled Ellen Terry when I wore a velvet
silk waistcoat—fleur-de-lys—a damaged
look is "in" this year—my forehead's dented—
the forceps grabbed too tight—a man at San
Juan beach felt my crotch when I was ten—
just a story I read during my recent dissolution—

97.   Orpheus (John Ashbery)

My life was mistitled *Imitation*—within it the word
skill misspelled—one "l"—*skil*—like *skol*—
or *shul*—I was a *skiled* lyre player—a *skiled*
hypnotist—I hopped over the *stile*—into
madness—beside haystacks—in Red Cloud—
my *skil* came in handy—at the apothecary's—
I drank aftershave—tasting like bubbly grape

pop—the flavor was misnamed *Concord*—
ice-pelted morbid town
where Adam and Eve are neighbors—smell
of Eve's pot roast down our tenement stairs—
she was good with her son—she read him stories
about pickles—Adam was in a pickle—'cause God
caught him staring at undressed Cain—

98.   Orpheus (Anouk Aimée)

He was a darling, stymied drip painter—
drip painting rewired his otherwise
damaged circuits—though he couldn't speak
he could paint—he carefully placed red next to green—
I, watching, mistook the green for gray—
his drips had a place in the new world order—
connected to the broken bank—the fallen stock—

was it too late for the monster to become
an artist?—he sulked in his frosty bedroom—
listening to "Night on Bald Mountain"—pretending
to conduct it—I curated his drip paintings—
ten million each—they sold like hotcakes—
with syrup—maple—in a dainty lady's-head pitcher—
beside a cup of hot milk flavored with hebona—

99.   Orpheus (Alfredo Germont)

My favorite paintings were Canalettos—
because my father was a gondolier with silver
booties and golden shirt and lion's-head belt
buckle—a cavaliere servente—beloved by doges—
I found him in a missing Canaletto's margin—
there—the man on a windy side canal—facing
away from the viewer—you can only see his back—

that's Dad—he also appears in Veronese—
and Van Eyck—he was a versatile model—
often appropriated for sordid uses—
Manet put him in a daub or two—
Degas used him as a ballet slipper—and I
as my gilt frame—here, see, the signed
canvas—his autograph's familial lavender—

100. Narcissus (Adam)

I ape the punished movements of the Earth—
as in the game of Simon Says—freeze tag—
I touch you—and you freeze—transformed to "it"—
my first friend, Tommy, was a fool—he spit
on another boy and called it impregnation—
as if a gravestone could describe its own decay—
we lost touch at age five—near San Andreas Fault—

he's back now—see him through this hole—
offered a peepshow view of evil
choose blindness—in my leper years I dared
eye the Lord—dared observe—from the vantage
of the spit-upon—my haggard Father drive—
a vaudeville virgin—away from His reward—
no orifice is a novice—Simon says—

101. Daphne (Oscar Wilde)

He handed me sticky rice buns, gray-toothed
mallards from my point of view—we hugged—
ancient nostril hairs sprouting—a distinguished
pianist—competition winner—his fiftieth
birthday—he courted me on Brompton Road—
I advertised his ass—and hers—chin versus
ass preoccupied me a fortnight—I gave the cake

to forty beggar boys playing Cage
etudes beneath cracked windowpanes
and drinking rain—not one drop false or true—
the sticky pianist wore hand splints—carpal
problems—ulner nerve—his adam's apple in disarray—
tho' surgery's impossible because he's psycho—
his Hapsburg nose flares downward—toward jet—

102. Daphne (Walt Whitman)

I wore garlic around my neck to ward off
realtors—they wanted my myth—at halfprice—
no way—*buy it fullprice if you want*—
that's what I told the realtor—the sieve—
crotchety—from Crete—she faxed me twice
each morning—*sell now*—her amber beads forgeries—
how can she run a business—with a leaking arm—

music leaks out—rock—dreadful stuff—
can't dance to it—it signals no epoch—
lacks a beat—her husband's false teeth rattle—
just like his novel—a failed fishing story—
about a detective eating boeuf bourguignon—
and mussel soup—with cracklings—totally Balzac—
also a forgery—and mortgaged, to boot—

103. Adonis (Mae West)

His breasts stuck out, snakes tattooed on each—
huge breasts for a ten-year-old—a Malaysian
prostitute I saw through a keyhole—
a chicken brothel—in New York—managed by
my godmother—staffed by angels—I lick
stamps—handle mailings—fetch lunch—
sweep—and give the prostitutes haircuts—

the "he" in question is my favorite—
boy—too bruised to merit a name—his mother
gave him up for adoption—his father's a steel
magnate—his sister a prima ballerina—you know
the family—they're famous—politically influential—
they own the waterfront—they lisp—they love science—
their specialty's marine life—talking dolphins—seals that read—

104.   Adonis (Violetta Valery)

I gave you a handsewn invitation to my bris—
gold leaf—RSVP—where were you—I'd planned it
around your lunchbreak—the fruit salad stunned—
on place St-Sulpice—near rue de Fleurus—
I smeared lanolin on my flesh—to cool—and cajole—
Madras tablecloth—finger bowls—soothsayers—
wasn't much sooth to say—I'll leave the operation
      undescribed—

foreskin memorable though inauthentic—
fifteen degrees Fahrenheit in the room—to anesthetize—
everyone chanted chorales—I watched it on TV—
in the coffee shop—closeups of the foreskin—
before and after—the newscaster compared it
to Jesus—later I remembered the pain—two kilos worth—
I bottled and sold it—elixir of foreskin—it heals—

105.   Orpheus (Elizabeth Taylor)

I sleep in the nativity pensione—Jerusalem—
my identity confused with the other god's—
red bumps between my knees and buttocks—
opaque glass panes separate me from Mary
who shuffles around the bathroom in fuzzy slippers
so as not to scratch her waxed floor—
why are there razors beside Mary's sink—

she sleeps below a pièta—a lump
in her mattress the hidden dowry—
for extra cash she raises rabbits—and makes
strawberry wine—gypsy with scarred calves—
she breathes stertorously, like a Portuguese
poet I once loved—she can barely see—
blind Mary—massacring her free-range rabbits—

106.   Orpheus (Wallace Stevens)

I don't mind being whipped by the overlarge
blonde great American novelist in the nextdoor
office—who stuns me with her electric cattle prod—
and wants me branded—a "Q" on my buttocks—
to show she owns me—I knew her scientist son—
we planned to become noted entomologists—
vivisectionists—bug posters on our bedroom doors—

what genes determined the novelist's
extreme height and her fear of the dark?—
the same genes I drink every breakfast
in my borscht—Gogol's old pal—
she translated him into Japanese haibun
and wears interlocked nostril rings as a world peace project—
novelists were taller before the bomb dropped—

107.   Orpheus (Gertrude Stein)

George Eliot is my daughter—a sickly girl with green
ringlets—I take her to the beach—we eat barbecue—
she is growing up to consider herself a princess—
this will be expensive—her handscrawled notes
are already worth a fortune—borderline—
she has no friends—on my wedding day she went
to the movies by herself—too bad I ruined her life—

years past—revealing my ripped-out heart's
irregular valves—I promised her a nuclear
family—plastic seat cushions—she spits
watermelon seeds into my palm—each seed
coated with starchy, costly saliva—George's—
she watches me roll the garden hose into a snake—
so I can damage the nascent crocuses—she watches without
        ire—

108. Orpheus (Frank Sinatra)

Rotten breakfast served in the pensione—fancy
ladies sipping tea—observing our gruel—
wondering why we don't complain—on the indolent
terrace—eyecontact with any poet you can name—
or any commentator—even the rats have legacies—
scampering from mezzanine to the new Italian wing—
I asked for lead weights to be placed on my toes—

so I wouldn't fly away—Grace agreed—
she intervened—*bastard you thrive on punishment*—
the difference between your first person
and third person narration is negligible—
Grace ran her fingers through my dead, limp curls—
I was her son for a day—her Lee cords unzipped—
rain boots resting in a puddle of goddess froth—

109. Orpheus (James Schuyler)

Old ladies curled in sleeping bags
beside the men's dry urinals—
accommodations poor—better than nothing—
Alice ate the crocuses—I managed her campaign
to consume every living flower—
I painted the stamens and she ate them—
morbid trash the trash collector said—and drove away—

Alice said *I hate you for fucking up my sister's head*—
sun penetrated her Limoges roof—
trying to appease I said *shall we see*
the King Tut exhibit—and then my father's chariot
crossed the sky—his birthday—and I was melting—
in pooled light—the slugged sister whispered
it's in bad taste to melt on a holiday—

110.   Orpheus (Egon Schiele)

Saw the following vagina the other day—
mine—it saved my life—
at the house of a renowned pornographer—
blown-up photograph on the wall—
my undeveloped vagina—or else the climactic
scene in a biblical pageant—taking place May 11—
the man who owned the vagina described it to me—

he'd never seen such a clean, oblivious version—
by accident I bit the pornographer's
finger—he yelped—*it's not funny* he said—
we cancelled our one hundred
eighty degree excursion—
we loved our stack of illegible exams—on Nero—
witness my ordinary vagina—just a father's—

111.   Orpheus (Elsa Schiaperelli)

I get choked up talking to you she said—
overdosing—the garbage truck backed up—she held
the raw stickshift—drew it from notch to notch—
broke my concentration—her hair smelled like
good crotch—no crotch is machinery—
I wrote the newspaper account of her obscenity trial—
medicated as a cue ball I woke

stumbling down the music library stairs—
toward the electrocution chamber—the Rameau
room—cembalo open—embellishments raised like antes—
I pushed myself onto the aesthete's electric
chair—and pulled the switch—as my political
Rosa Luxemburg told me to do when we excommunicated—
each X a lush communiqué on her river bank—

112. Orpheus (Samson)

O siren you sway me no longer
I sang to the bun in my hand—my sugar roll—
bosom pal—coated with molasses—shaped
like a dormer window out which a crazy
Sicilian shouted *fuckwad* at me though
my ears were cotton-swaddled shut—
tied to the mast I drank tea with milk—

I loved seafaring—I had a knack for navigation—
I slept in the ship dungeon—while cannibals
prepared dinner—a small boy was hors d'oeuvres—
his legs in white sauce—I chewed boned
boy—seafood delicacy—he cried out—
he wasn't dead yet—sauce smothered his lament—
I had no sympathy with the consumed boy—

113. Echo (Saint Teresa)

Alice hacked into a mottled handkerchief—
at least you're not tubercular I said—a lie—
I've been dying for a decade she protested—and strode
toward my gelded folio—it contained
oblivion—a recipe for prune cake—
crumbs that pleased the cupbearer—I'd left
the page unfinished, years ago—did she mend

that breach—or has she changed it into kine?—
O Paris—the thousand stairs I climbed to reach
your fabled air—I stopped before I broached
the final step—as if to knock were indiscreet—
but when I woke—Alice's zircon car—parked
on the Stygian street—had died—and my cleft
song—mine and not mine—occupied the zone

114.   Echo (Saint Sebastian)

with balm—*we're living in an occupied zone*
these days, my friend she said—*Gertrude sends love*
but don't pay attention to the words—
just put your nose between the cracks in the lore—
remember the wild rose soaps
we left for you in the guest loo—we didn't want you to feel
abandoned—alone in the rear wing—so we poured

starlight in your ewer—when it cracked open
you were sloppy—you didn't sponge the nighttable—
our system left a stain—we know you hate
to open wide—but we think you're ready now
to take the radiance in your mouth—ore
you've long avoided—it goes by many names—
all are public—all are yours—

> *love—land—luxe—loose—*

loss—lad—lisp—lass—lap—lab—lip—last—lust—lack—
> *law—Loire—*